D1593446

JEWISH PREACHING

BY THE SAME AUTHOR

Jewish Prayer

A Guide to Rosh Ha-Shanah

A Guide to Yom Kippur

Jewish Values

Studies in Talmudic Logic and Methodology

The Palm Tree of Deborah
(Translated from the Hebrew of Moses Cordovero, with
Introduction Notes)

Tract on Ecstasy
(Translated from the Hebrew of Dobh Baer of Lubavitch,
with Introduction and Notes)

Principles of the Jewish Faith:
An Analytical Study

A Jewish Theology

The Talmudic Argument

Helping with Inquiries

God, Torah, Israel

Religion and the Individual

In production for 2004

Their Heads in Heaven:
Unfamiliar Aspects of Hasidism

Judaism and Theology:
Essays on the Jewish Religion

Rabbinic Thought in the Talmud

JEWISH PREACHING
Homilies and Sermons

LOUIS JACOBS

VALLENTINE MITCHELL
LONDON • PORTLAND, OR

BM
730
.J33
2004

First published in 2004 in Great Britain by
VALLENTINE MITCHELL & CO. LTD
Premier House, 112–114 Station Road, Edgware, Middlesex HA8 7BJ

and in the United States of America by
VALLENTINE MITCHELL
c/o ISBS,
920 NE 58th Avenue, Suite 300, Portland, OR 97213-3786 USA

Copyright © Louis Jacobs 2004

British Library Cataloguing in Publication Data
have been applied for

Library of Congress Cataloging in Publication Data
have been applied for

ISBN 0 85303 561 X (cloth)
0 85303 565 2 (paper)

All rights reserved. No part of this publication may be reproduced in any form or by any means, electronic, mechanical, photocopying, reading or otherwise, without the prior permission of Vallentine Mitchell & Co. Ltd.

Printed in Great Britain by
MPG Books Ltd, Bodmin, Cornwall

Contents

For my lovely little great-granddaughters
Ella and Hannah Lucie Jacobs and Jordan
Hannah Green

Preface

A word of explanation, not to say of excuse, is called for as to why a preacher from various pulpits during almost sixty years should have decided just now to publish a series of extrapolations of Scriptural verses. First, there is the natural desire of an elderly rabbi, as time appears to be more fleeting than ever before, to rescue from oblivion his efforts in this direction. The truth is that, while I have always tried to prepare my sermons fully before delivery, I have never been at home in using a manuscript and have spoken extemporarily for better or for worse. However, thanks to invitations from Jewish journals, especially the *Jewish Chronicle*, I have published sermonic ideas in print, some of which are published in this volume. These printed homilies extend over a period of around fifty years. It would not have been appropriate simply to reproduce these as they stood. Times have changed rapidly in this area as well, so that a thorough revision has been necessary and much new material has been added.

A homily differs from a sermon in several respects. The sermon is more personal, more spontaneous, has greater flexibility and is far more direct than the homily; naturally so since, in the sermon, a live audience is addressed. Every preacher is aware that he is speaking face to face with his congregation. He looks at them, or should do, while he is preaching. In a subtle way they participate creatively in his message by the way they receive it. A yawn or a sense that he is boring on (in both senses of the word) is sufficient to throw him off his stride. A touch of humour, even an occasional joke, is essential if he is to hold their interest. An element of passion is also an integral part of the sermon, though this can be overdone all too easily. 'What will happen if he gets out?' as the little girl remarked to her mother when listening to a fiery preacher, gesticulating in a high, enclosed pulpit.

A homily is more formal, more structured and more contrived. When it is on a Scriptural verse it should come close to Biblical exegesis, albeit in subjective rather than objective form. Your homilist is not saying: 'This is the true meaning of the verse.' That is a matter for objective scholars who have to convince their peers of the correctness of their arguments. The homilist is saying something like this: 'It seems to me, from my own experience and from my study of the Torah, that the following idea or ideas can be extrapolated from the verse so as to bear a contemporary significance.'

In this book I present one or more, comparatively short, homilies on each of the weekly portions of the Torah with a few on 'Ethics of the Fathers', the wonderful early Rabbinic work now part of the liturgy for the summer months. Jewish preachers, ancient as well as modern, have generally based their weekly message on these sources. It goes without saying that these are Jewish homilies, addressed chiefly to Jewish readers and therefore particularistic in their stance. Yet the universalistic and individualistic elements in Judaism have not been overlooked. It is hoped that non-Jewish readers will also find points of interest and comparison. Other books I have compiled have their full quota of documentation of sources but I confess that it has been a relief to publish a work free from what has been dubbed 'foot and note disease'. The non-clap-happy congregations it has been my privilege to serve would never have dreamed of calling out 'Amen' to my utterances and have been very sparing even with an occasional *yasher koah*. Perhaps, however, readers of the book will visit some of my effusions, at least, with a touch of the latter.

PART ONE
INTRODUCTION

— 1 —

Introduction

> The preacher should not make his sermon too long in order not to burden the congregation. However, he should not make his sermon too short either, for it is not right to trouble the people by having brought them to hear something which is too brief. In order to preserve his health, the preacher should go immediately to rest after he has delivered the sermon. He should drink a little fine wine or chicken soup.
>
> Jacob Zahalon 1630–93, *Guide to Preachers*

Israel Bettan's *Studies in Jewish Preaching: Middle Ages* (Hebrew Union College Press, Cincinnati, 1939) is still the best account of pre-modern Jewish preaching. First showing how the sermon proper developed from the *derashah* in Talmudic times, Bettan surveys the works of the most famous Jewish preachers from the thirteenth to the eighteenth centuries, although we do not have their actual sermons, only their homiletical Hebrew compilations, that is to say, sermonic themes expressed in literary rather than verbal form. Bettan's chapter headings are sufficient in themselves to point to the great variety of the preachers and the gradual evolution of the earlier sermon to pave the way for the new sermonic thrust in the early nineteenth century: 'Jacob Anatoli: A Thirteenth-century Liberal'; 'Bahya Ben Asher: A Practical Mystic'; 'Isaac Arama: The Preacher's Preacher'; 'Judah Moscato: Child of the Renaissance'; 'Azariah Figo: Critic of Life'; 'Ephraim Luntshitz: Champion of Change'; 'Jonathan Eybeshitz: Passionate Pleader'. The following works presage in a similar way the different mood of the nineteenth-century preacher.

David Darshan of Cracow (sixteenth century) wrote *Shir Ha-Maalot L'David* and *Ktav Hitnatzzelut L'Darshanim* (Song of the

Steps and In Defense of Preachers), translated and annotated by H. G. Perelmuter, Hebrew Union College Press, Cincinnati, 1984. David was the first itinerant Jewish preacher whose sermons were published; an amulet writer, and an artist (the jacket illustration is a copy of his illustration to a Kabbalistic manuscript depicting Rabbi Akiba's ascent to Heaven – the picture of Rabbi Akiba gives us some idea of what a Polish Rabbi of the time looked like). Perelmuter describes David as a 'Renaissance man'. This is hardly correct; judging by the examples he gives, his sermons are of the complicated pilpulistic type. Nevertheless, the very form and content of this book (it is incidentally in rhymed prose) show that even among his Polish contemporaries new winds were blowing.

A Rabbi more deserving of the title 'a Renaissance man' is the seventeenth-century Italian scholar, Jacob Zahalon, author of *Or Ha-Darshanim* (Guide for Preachers), translated by Henry Adler Sosland (The Jewish Theological Seminary of America, New York, 1987). This is the first preacher's manual ever to be published. This guide for preachers, novel in itself, has a remarkably modern tone. Zahalon has sections on the subject and content of the sermon; on its quality, length and manner of introduction; on the proper use of the voice and on the manner of speaking and on the use of gestures; on the purpose of preaching sermons and on their proper conclusion; on concern for the preacher's health as a means to more effective preaching.

Apart from the above, the only work of advice to preachers did not appear until the publication of A. Cohen's *Jewish Homiletics*, (Jewish Chronicle Publications, London, 1937). Dr Cohen was lecturer in homiletics at the College. Among other matters, Dr Cohen offers advice to preachers on the homiletical use of the Bible, the non-Biblical sources of homiletics, on words, on ideas and illustrations, sermon composition and delivery.

Part of the aim of Zunz's most famous work, *Gottesdienstliche Vortraege der Juden* (1832), was to demonstrate, when this was challenged by the Prussian government (under the influence of Orthodox groups who saw the sermon in the vernacular as the beginnings of Reform), that preaching is not an innovation but an ancient Jewish institution. While this is true, the traditional *derashah* was, in fact, replaced in the nineteenth century by a new type of Jewish sermon, the *Predigt*, as it was called in Germany. There were a number of important changes in language, style and content which, first in Germany and then in other European countries, gave a completely new cast to the sermon. This new type of sermon was delivered in the vernacular and, unlike the occasional *derashah*, it was a regular feature of the service. It sought to express Jewish values in a contemporary idiom and in the thought-patterns of the day. Woven around one central theme, the modern sermon developed in orderly fashion, without academic digressions on the texts quoted, emphasizing edification rather than pure instruction. Although the early-nineteenth-century preachers in Germany were not rabbis, preaching, instead of being relegated to a special functionary, eventually became the preserve of the Rabbi and one of his most important duties in Western countries. Among the well-known preachers in nineteenth-century Germany were: Eduard Kley, Gotthold Salomon, Abraham Geiger, Samuel Holdheim, Jehiel Michael Sachs, Samson Raphael Hirsch and David Einhorn; and in the twentieth century: Siegmund Maybaum, Nehemia Anton Nobel and Leo Baeck.

Dr A. Altmann, a great scholar and no mean preacher himself (I often heard him preach when he served as communal Rabbi in Manchester), wrote on the history of early Jewish preaching (ed., *Studies in Nineteenth-Century Jewish Intellectual History*, Harvard University Press, 1964, pp. 65–116), showing the influence of the Protestant pulpit on the development of the modern Jewish sermon. The early German preachers consciously modelled their sermons on the patterns of Christian homiletics and used Christian guides to the art of preaching. Even Isaac Noah Mannheimer, the most outstanding nineteenth-century preacher who pleaded for a closer link with the Jewish homiletical tradition, admitted that 'we, as pupils and disciples, as novices in the art of preaching, which we have been practising only a little while, can learn a great deal from the masters of the art, and we have gratefully to accept every guidance and instruction offered to us in their schools. Zunz, in his brief career as a preacher at the New Synagogue in Berlin (1820–22), was influenced by Schleiermacher. It is even on record that the most popular Christian preachers of the time, such as Ritschl and Schleiermacher, used to hear the young preachers at Israel Jacobson's temple in Berlin and give them, after the sermon, 'manifest hints and directives'.

A reaction soon set in. There was a persistent demand for a truly Jewish homiletics, arguing, in Mannheimer's words, that 'it is always better to feed on one's own resources than to live from alms'. However, generally speaking, the reaction in the nineteenth-century a mounted only to a greater use of rabbinic, especially midrashic, material as exemplified in the sermons of the illustrious preacher Adolf Jellinek in Vienna. Jellinek's preaching attracted many of the intellectuals of the day who, in their quest for Jewish identity, needed the reassurance that Judaism was supremely worthwhile and still capable of making important contributions. Jellinek was fond of preaching that too many were saying: 'Now Israel's eyes were dim with age, he could not see' (Genesis 48: 10), whereas the truth was that Moses still spoke and God still answered him in thunder (Exodus 19:19). Jellinek's methods and strong Jewish emphasis influenced Jewish preaching everywhere. A later occupant of Jellinek's pulpit, Hirsch (Zevi) Peretz Chajes, for example, preached to a bar mitzvah the story of the woman whose vessels were miraculously replenished by the oil (2 Kings 4:1–7). The never-ending power of Judaism is always available if only Jews will provide the vessels with which to contain it. No matter how great the Jew's spiritual demands, Judaism is capable of satisfying them.

Tobias Goodman is credited with being the first Jew to preach in the English language. Two of Goodman's printed sermons are: *A Sermon on the Universally Regretted Death of the Most Illustrious Princess Charlotte*, preached on Wednesday, 19 November 1817, at the synagogue, Denmark Court, London (the first sermon to be both delivered and printed in English) and *A Sermon Occasioned by the Demise of Our Late Venerable Sovereign, King George the Third*, preached on Wednesday, 18 February 1820, at the same synagogue (A. Barnett, *The Western Synagogue Through Two Centuries*, 1961, pp.48–51). In December 1828, a Committee of Elders was appointed at the Bevis Marks Sephardi Synagogue in London, to inquire into the best means of elevating the tone of public services. Among their recommendations was that an English sermon based on a text taken from Scripture should be delivered every Saturday afternoon. Before delivery, every sermon should be examined by a committee of three elders for statements contrary to Jewish doctrines or hostile to the institutions of the country (J. Piccioto, *Sketches of Anglo-Jewish History*, 1956, pp. 318–20). This would not be permissible nowadays. In the USA, preaching in the English language was introduced much later. Some preachers, like the Reform Rabbi David Einhorn, preferred to give sermons in their native German. Einhorn declared: 'Where the German language is banned, there the reform of Judaism is nothing more than a brilliant gloss, a decorated doll, without heart, without soul, which the proudest and the most splendid theories cannot succeed in infusing with life.' Nevertheless, the sermon in English won the day, as was inevitable. The English sermon was developed to a fine art by such preachers as Simeon Singer, Morris Joseph, Chief Rabbi Joseph Herman Hertz, Israel Mattuck, A. A. Green, Abraham Cohen and Ephraim Levine in England; Stephen S. Wise, Israel Herbert Levinthal, Abba Hillel Silver, Solomon Goldman and Solomon Bennett Freehof in the USA. Two annual collections of sermons in English were published by the Rabbinical Council of America (Orthodox) from 1943, and from 1954, the collection by rabbis of all three groups as *Best Jewish Sermons*, edited by Saul I. Teplitz.

In Eastern Europe the older type of *derashah*, delivered in Yiddish by the *maggid*, still predominated, but certain new features manifested themselves even here. The winds of change in the Jewish world moved the *maggidim* to find a rather more sophisticated approach. Preaching in Yiddish became directed to the needs of the individual as well as the community. The Haskalah movement was frequently attacked by the *maggidim* with the weapons of public oratory. With the rise of Zionism, many of its opponents used the same weapons to combat it, while others, sympathetic to Zionism, preached the love of the Holy Land and the legitimacy of Jewish nationalistic aspirations. Professor Selig Brodetsky, addressing Jewish audiences in the East End of London on Zionism, would ask them first: 'Do you want me to speak in English or in Yiddish?' 'English,' was the usual reply. 'Yiddish we know already.'

In point of fact, there emerged in East European centres a new type of nationalistic preacher given the name *mattif* ('speaker', Micah 2:11), to distinguish him from the old type of *maggid*. Under the influence of the Lithuanian Musar movement, with its strong moralistic thrust, the *derashah* began to place greater emphasis on ethical matters. The hell-fire preaching of R. Moshe Yitzhak, the Kelmer Maggid (1828–1900), the most popular of the folk preachers, was directed largely against dishonesty in business and general dishonest conduct (D. Katz: *Tenuat H-Musar*, vol. 2, 1958, pp. 395–407). Many of the *maggidim* went to the USA, England and South Africa, where their preaching was directed against the widespread desecration of the Sabbath and neglect of the dietary laws, abuses unknown in their native countries. *Maggidim* still flourish in the State of Israel, but there has been little development of the sermon in Hebrew and the rabbi-preacher is virtually unknown

there as a regular and respected synagogue functionary. Among
the Yiddish preachers of renown were: Hayyim Zundel Macoby,
known as the Kaminitzer Maggid, J. L. Lazarov, Z. H. Masliansky,
Isaac Nissenbaum, M. A. Amiel, Zalman Sorotzkin and Zeev Gold.
Amiel, Rabbi of Antwerp and later Chief Rabbi of Tel-Aviv, was
well-read in general and in Jewish philosophy, and some of his
sermons are really theological essays in the manner of those of
Anatoli and Arama, mentioned above, in the Middle Ages.

The Revd Simeon Singer, in 'Where the Clergy Fail', an address
delivered to young preachers on 17 January 1904 (*Lectures and
Addresses*, 1908, pp. 203–25), describes the aim of the Jewish preacher thus: 'to teach the word of God to their brethren, young and old;
to help them to the perception of the highest truths of religion; to
uplift their souls out of the rut of the common, the sordid, in life;
to speak a message of comfort to the sorrowing, of hope to the
despondent, of counsel to the perplexed, of courage to the strug-
gling and aspiring'. This lengthy sentence in good English prose is
typical of the style of the Anglo-Jewish clergy (note the term) one
hundred years ago, when the Rabbis, even if they had *semikhah*, as
did Singer himself, had the title of 'Reverend' and were 'minister-
preachers'. The sole Rabbi was the Chief Rabbi. It is all an echo
from the past. Yet Singer's advice, though no doubt influenced by
the patterns and customs of the Church of England, was acceptable
everywhere as the ideal. The whole is based on the belief that the
art of preaching can be taught. We have seen earlier that this was
the belief of Zahalon in seventeenth-century Rome. In this
conviction, the major rabbinic seminaries have departments of
homiletics. Siegmund Maybaum taught homiletics at the
Hochschule in Berlin, Israel Bettan at Hebrew Union College,
Mordecai Kaplan at the Jewish Theological Seminary, and Abraham
Cohen at Jews' College. The popularity of such courses depended
naturally on the skills of the teacher. Yet, to this day, there is a tendency among students at rabbinical seminaries, and among many
of the teachers, to look upon homiletics as a branch of Jewish learning inferior to the other branches and as a subject that requires few
qualifications or little training. It is often said, to the detriment of
pulpit work, 'Almost anyone, with an amount, however small, of
Jewish knowledge, can get up and deliver a sermon.'

The modern Jewish sermon is usually based on a text chosen
from the *sidra* or the *haftarah* read in the synagogue on the day
when the sermon is delivered. Books of the Bible which are not

read in public, such as Job and Proverbs, rarely furnish texts for sermons, though they may be quoted in support of a position the preacher adopts. Normally the sermon is delivered after the Sefer Torah has been returned to the Ark. While the note of exhortation is never entirely absent from the sermon, many preachers, nowadays, prefer to use the sermon chiefly as a means of instruction, imparting infomation about Jewish faith, history and teachings. The length of the sermon varies from preacher to preacher, but on the average is about twenty minutes. Preaching from a prepared manuscript is the rule for some preachers, while others prefer to speak extemporaneously. Dr Altmann, in an address to preachers, made the point that once you have got it down on paper freshness and spontaneity are lost; but it is recognized that adequate preparation is essential for every type of preaching. A sermon falls somewhere in between a casual talk and a lecture, every detail of which is present before the ascent of the podium. Oratory has now generally yielded to an easier, more relaxed conversational tone. Few preachers would today follow the example of Leo Baeck, of whom it was said that he never used the personal pronoun 'I' in the pulpit. On the other hand, few would adopt an overfamiliar colloquial style like the preacher who said: 'The prophet Isaiah said and I heartily agree with him'!

Sermon illustrations are taken from the personal experience of the preacher, Jewish history, the Midrash, natural science and psychology, and, latterly, Hasidic lore. L. I. Newman's *Hasidic Anthology* (1934) and Martin Buber's *Tales of the Hasidim* (1947–84) have come to serve as a rich source fior sermon illustrations. Quotations from secular literature are used to develop a theme. In a typical outline of a sermon on Kol Nidre by Milton Steinberg (*Sermons*, ed. B. Mandelbaum, 1954, pp. 58–63) there are references to the Geonim, Walter Pater, Tennyson, Leibnitz, Omar Khayyam and W. L. Phelps. Louis Rabinowitz (*Out of the Depths*, 1954, pp. 332–5) builds a Kol Nidrei sermon around a poem by the modern Hebrew writer Zalman Shneur. In a Day of Atonement sermon by Israel H. Levinthal (*Steering or Drifting – Which?*, 1928, pp. 128–35) there are quotations from Judah Halevi, the Talmud, the prayer book, a Christian legend, folk language, the Bible and the Midrash. Preachers in the USA often take for their theme a book, film or play that has received much attention for its treatment of some moral or religious question. Some sermons conclude with a prayer. This and other pulpit pretensions were, however, severely criticized by

Franz Rosenzweig in his scathing attack on preaching entitled 'Sermonic Judaism' (N. N. Glatzer: *Franz Rosenzweig*, 1953, pp. 247–50).

The chosen text and the way it is treated depend on the individual preferences of the preacher but, judging by published sermons, certain themes are constant. Each of the festivals, for example, has its particular message so far as the preacher is concerned. The theme of Passover is freedom; of Shavuot, Jewish education (in Orthodox pulpits, the immutability of the Torah); of Sukkot trust in God and thankfulness for His bounty; of Hanukkah spiritual light; of Purim Jewish peoplehood; of Rosh Hashanah the need for renewal; and on the Day of Atonement sin and atonement. The wise preacher on Yom Kippur will resist that too -strong type of admonition which panders to the masochism of some 'congregants and the *Schadenfreude* of others who are only too ready to declare: 'He gave them what for.' In addition to the weekly Sabbath sermon the rabbi preaches on the special occasions in the life of his congregation: anniversaries, weddings, funerals, installation of officers, at bar mitzvahs, and at his/her own induction. A number of rabbinic manuals contain sermonic material in capsule form for the Rabbi's use on special occasions (e.g., H. E. Goldin: *Ha-Madrikh*, 1938).

The modern Jewish sermon frequently addresses itself to particular problems that agitate the Jewish community as well as to wider issues of universal import. There is much discussion on the extent to which politics should be introduced, but few Jewish preachers accept a total ban on political questions. In a famous *New Yorker* cartoon, a bishop advises a young curate: 'My boy, you will do fine as long as you keep off controversial topics such as politics and religion'! There are numerous instances of rabbis seeking to influence their congregations either when a topic is a source of controversy within the community or when they feel that widely held views are contrary to Jewish teaching. Themes treated in the contemporary pulpit are: the supposed conflict between religion and science, the role of the State of Israel, the permissive society, intermarriage, Jewish education, war and peace, social injusticeracial discrimination, the taking of drugs, on the 'Death of God' movement, fair housing, the use and abuse of wealth, the estrangement of the Jewish intellectual from Judaism, recreation, the need to care for the hungry and oppressed, the relation of Judaism to other religions. The 1986 edition of *Best Jewish Sermons*, published in the USA, contains sermons on these and similar themes by representativesof Orthodox, Reform and Conservative Rabbis who, notwithstanding their organizational differences, show close agreement when dealing with such wider themes. Rabbis have fought to free the pulpit from control by the leaders of the congregation. When Stephen Wise was being considered for the influential post of Rabbi of Temple Emmanuel in New York, Louis Marshall, the president, held that in controversial matters the pulpit must remain under the control of the trustees. Wise refused to consider the post under such conditions and eventually founded the Free Synagogue to uphold the principle of pulpit liberty.

In nineteenth-century America the slavery issue was addressed, from the Jewish pulpit. Morris J. Raphall preached that slavery is a divinely ordained institution, since it is mentioned in the Bible. David Einhorn, however, attacked slavery from the pulpit as 'the greatest crime against God'. As a result, his life was placed in jeopardy and on 22 April 1861, Einhorn and his family were secretly escorted out of Baltimore.

With the rise of the Reform movement, the issue of Reform was hotly debated from the pulpit. A favourite text for the Reform sermon, used by Geiger and others, was: 'One generation passeth away, and another generation cometh, but the earth aideth for ever' (Ecclesiastes 1:4). The 'earth' represents the essential, unchanging spirit of Judaism, which must be interpreted by each generation in the light of its own needs and insights. Such an interpretation was dismissed by the Orthodox as far-fetched homiletics, contrary, moreover, to the doctrine that the Torah is immutable. For the Orthodox, if the 'earth' is made to represent the Torah, it remains unchanging through all the generations that come and go. It often happened, in fact, that the same set of texts would be used by both Orthodox and Reform preachers in support of their respective positions. The 'wicked son' of the Passover Haggadah was, for the Orthodox preacher, the Reform Jew who asks: 'What is this service for you?' For the Reform preacher the son who represented the Reform point of view was the 'wise son' who was ready to ask all the intelligent questions demanded by the new age.

On this topic of Orthodox and Reform preaching it can be noted that Chief Rabbi N. M. Adler preached in London, on the second day of Passover in 1868, a sermon against the abolition of the second days of festivals in the Diaspora, a matter which at that time had begun to be an issue between Orthodoxy and Reform. His son and successor, Hermann Adler, at the beginning of the twentieth century, refused to permit a synagogue under his jurisdiction, the Hampstead Synagogue, to appoint Morris Joseph as minister-preacher, because Joseph had published views 'at variance with traditional Judaism'. Joseph had written that he did not look forward to the restoration of sacrifices in the Temple of the future and, therefore, could not honestly pray for this to happen. Solomon Schechter, at that time living in Cambridge, pointed out that if doctrines were to become the test of a minister, then the greatest names in Jewish learning – Zunz, Graetz, Herzfeld, Joel, Gotthold, Solomon, Rapoport and others – would never have been permitted to preach in a United Synagogue (R. Apple: *The Hampstead Synagogue*, 1967, pp. 23–7). Chief Rabbi J. H. Hertz preached a series of sermons, *Affirmations of Judaism*. (1927), attacking the new Liberal movement founded by C. G. Montefiore and others. Hertz made no concessions, but why should he have done? Pulpit ire and fire can be overdone, but the most effective of preachers are those who occasionally, at least, get excited. Of Hertz it was said that he preferred the way of peace if there was no other.

THEOLOGICAL PREACHING

So far in this essay I have tried to give a brief, objective account of preaching with particular emphasis on what has happened and is happening in this field in modern times. Now I want to be a little more subjective and consider the question of theological preaching. Having spent years studying theology, I naturally demonstrate my bias. What follows is largely a repeat of a lecture I gave to the Rabbinical Assembly of America, entitled *The Pulpit as an Instrument of Theological Teachings* (*Proceedings of the Rabbinical Assembly*, New York, 1969, pp. 9–24). The lecture was received quite well by my colleagues of the Rabbinical Assembly (Conservative) but was subjected to criticism, of which I have taken note.

Of all the different types of sermon the theological is undoubtedly the most neglected in the synagogue. One of the reasons for this neglect is the unfortunate notion that it is somehow unJewish to do theology at all, so that 'Jewish theology' is considered to be a contradiction in terms. A widespread Midrashic (Jerusalem

Talmud, *Hagigah* 1:7) quote is: 'God says: "Would that they had forsaken Me and kept My Torah."' This is, needless to say, a misquotation, since the Midrash clearly does not mean to imply that God wants us not to think about Him. The meaning is rather that God is prepared, as it were, to settle for uninformed, self-seeking observance of the Torah (*shelo lishmah*) because such is the intrinsic power of the Torah that even this will eventually lead Israel to Him. 'The light she contains will restore them to the good.' To see theological thinking and discussion as an offence insults the memory of Saadiah and Maimonides, Cordovero and the Ari, Shneur Zalman of Liady and Hayyim of Volozhyn and, in modern times, Moses Mendelsohn, Schechrer, Rabbi Kook, Kaufmann Kohlrt, Samuel S. Cohon, Buber, Rosenzweig and Leo Baeck.

Nor is it true that theology is a harmless but irrelevant pastime, a luxury we can ill afford in our age when so many practical problems press in on us. Even on pragmatic grounds, theology is important because how Jews lead their lives depends on how they conceive of the purpose of Jewish existence. 'Show me a man's philosophy,' said Chesterton, 'and I'll show you the man.' Is it not correct, for instance, that all the divisions among religious Jews on the scope and obligation of Jewish observances depend ultimately on differing views regarding a basic theological question, the meaning of revelation?

It is also a mistake to imagine that Jews who come to synagogue and listen to sermons have no interest in theology. The opposite is much nearer to the truth; that in an average Jewish congregation nowadays one is likely to find a number of hungry souls who are merely irritated by appeals to Jewish pride or loyalty but who have an intense desire to know what Judaism is, who are well aware of what Judaism would have them do, but are puzzled as to what it is that Judaism would have them believe.

Theological instruction is, consequently, a legitimate and necessary function of the synagogue pulpit. The wise preacher will, of course, vary the type of fare he offers. Too rich a diet of theology, as of any other pulpit topic, will produce an imbalance and succeed only in giving people spiritual indigestion.

There is, however, a difficulty particularly inherent in theological preaching. The sermon is not a lecture. A sermon has rightly been described as 'truth mediated through personality'. It is the preacher's task to convey to his congregation how he personally sees Jewish life. It should be far removed from a detached, academic exercise. And yet theology, by its very nature, is abstract, metaphysical, elusive. Theology appears to be concerned much more with the making of maps with which to explore the unknown than with the existential situation of Jews in the here and now. The 'Queen of the Sciences' is not easily coerced from her regal aloofness to engage in full participation in the hurly-burly of the world of our normal experience.

The difficulty can be met if the preacher is always on the lookout for definite, concrete experiences in his own life and that of his congregation to serve both as pegs on which to hang theological ideas and as actual illustrations of how these ideas are to be used. A consideration of the doctrine of the Hereafter becomes arresting if delivered at a sermon during the Yizkor service when each one is thinking of his departed and reflecting perhaps on his or her own mortality. If the newspapers carry a report of an uninformed attack on Jewry or, for that matter, of too fulsome praise, then is the time to preach on the Chosen People idea. The publication of the latest bestseller on 'the death of God' is as opportune a time as any for discussion in the pulpit of the Jewish doctrine of the living God. Actual questions put to the rabbi by college students, for example, or even by little children in the Hebrew school ('who made God?') can serve as springboards for theological preaching. A Jewish mother told me of a conversation she overheard between her two little boys aged five and seven. The younger boy asked his brother: 'Do you believe in God?' The older boy replied: 'I did when I was your age but I have grown out of it now.' If, God fobid, a disaster such as an earthquake occurs, the Rabbis will be expected to comment on how they cope as Jews with the problem of pain and evil in the universe. (Here a note of warning should be sounded. I would not myself speak on theology when a member of the congregation has passed away, but confine pulpit references in that instance to praise of the deceased and the severity of the loss sustained. While thinking of a particular person known to the congregation and whose relatives are there in the synagogue, it is virtually impossible to speak on the problem of suffering without appearing to vindicate God at the expense of the tears of this particular bereaved family.)

As for the techniques of thelogical preaching, these will naturally differ from Rabbi to Rabbi. Many of the homilies in this book are theological in nature, but here I want to present a further number of general suggestions for theological preaching.

A sermon on the nature of God describing how the Neo-

Platonic distinction between God as He is in Himself and God as He manifests Himself to His creatures was adopted by the medieval Jewish thinkers. (I am not suggesting that terms like 'Neo-Platonic' should be used in a sermon. If name-dropping ever has a place it is not in the pulpit.) Reference can be made to the Zoharic interpretation (*Zohar* 1:1b) of: 'Lift up your eyes on high, and see who hath created these?' (Isaiah 40:26). For the *Zohar Who?* (*mi*) is *deus absconditus*, of whom only the question: '*Who is He?*, can be asked with no answer forthcoming to the inquiring mind of finite humans. *These* (*elleh*) refers to God in manifestation, whose glory fills the earth – the world of of division and multiplicity, of diverse creatures and complex forms of being, through which, in Von Hugel's phrase, He can be apprehended but not comprehended. One might even go on to consider the very radical Kabbalistic view that God as He is in Himself (*En Sof*) is not mentioned at all in the Bible (so elevated is that aspect of Deity above all human thought and language) except by hint and that *elohim* (*mi* and *elleh* combined), the God of vital religion, *deus revelatus*, is brought into being, as it were as part of the divine self-revelatory process. This is one way of trying to cope with the problem of reconciling the 'God of the philosophers' with the 'God of Abraham, Isaac and Jacob'. Such ideas can be developed further or criticized according to the individual bent of the preacher and the intellectual capacity of the congregation. I have found, and I am sure the majority of my colleagues have found, the intellectual level of Jews who come to synagogue to be exceedingly high.

Pursuing this line further, one might preach on: 'For man may not see Me and live' (Exodus 33: 20) and contrast this verse, as the Rabbis (*Yevamot* 49b) did, with the verse in Isaiah (6:1): 'I saw the Lord.' The Rabbinic distinction is between the lucid speculum and the dim speculum. Rashi adds the subtle explanation that Moses knew that, through the clear glass, in reality, one cannot see but Isaiah, who saw 'through a glass darkly', deluded himself that he could see. The idea can be developed that the more gifted human beings are with spiritual insight the greater their reluctance to talk about God's nature. For Maimonides (*Guide* 1:59) the difference between the wisest of men and ordinary folk is that the former know so much better how little can be said about the divine.

In preaching on faith in God, it is helpful to point out that many deeply religious persons have been troubled by doubts and that there is nothing to be ashamed of in being so troubled. Nahman of

Bratzlav even goes so far as to say that man is bound to have doubts since this is endemic to the human condition, for man is a finite creature incapable of grasping the Infinite. A powerful text from Nahman's writings is his comment on: 'So the people remained at a distance, while Moses approached the thick cloud where God was' (Exodus 20:18). The 'people', those who lack faith's courage, recoil as soon as they are faced with religious problems. They remain at a distance. Moses, however, the heroic 'knight of faith', presses on to find God in the darkness itself. One of the best treatments of this whole question of tension in the line of faith is to be found in the sermon notes of Milton Steinberg ('Discovery of God' in: *From the Sermons of Rabbi Milton Steinberg*, ed. Bernard Mandelbaum, New York, 1954, pp. 73-84). Incidentally, Milton Steinberg's writings contain a good deal of theological material, attractively presented, which can be used by the Rabbi. Otherwise, there is little enough material upon which the theological preacher can draw. One work which should be mentioned and which deserves to be better known is the theological, Hebrew anthology, *Ha-Elohut*, by Israel Konovitz (New York, 1905). Solomon Schechter's *Aspects of Rabbinic Theology* (New York, 1961); Montefiore and Loewe's *A Rabbinic Anthology* (London, 1938) and A. Cohen's *Everyman's Talmud* are also useful aides.

A part of faith's tension is the need to affirm both the inescapable nature of religious commitment and human free and willing choice. On the one hand humans cannot escape the 'hound of heaven'. Jonah takes a ship to Tarshish to evade his responsibility (this would be equivalent to somone taking a jet from New York to San Franciso when he has a duty to perform in London), but God does not allow him to escape. Yet, if this aspect of the matter alone is stressed, God is conceived of as a celestial puppet-master who moves people as He wills, with them playing no part in their decisions. Many people do, in fact, tend to think of God in this way. However, on the deeper level the meaning is that man's ultimate happiness and self-fulfilment lie in obedience to God's law, and this is demanded of him not as something foreign but as something intrinsic to his nature. Jews can respond willingly to the call of duty because the obligations of Judaism are natural expressions of the deepest longings of man created in God's image. In the verse from the Evening Prayer, the Israelites *'willingly* accepted God's sovereignty'. If, according to the Midrash, God compels the Israelites to accept the Torah by threatening them with the mountain suspended over their heads, their eventual response is: we will do and will hear. Bahya Ibn Asher notes that the Hebrew word *yimlokh* in the verse 'The Lord will reign for ever and ever' (Exodus 15:18) is written defectively (without a *vav*) to imply that God is, as it were, deficient in the sterner aspects of sovereignty. He is not to be conceived of as a despot forcing unwilling subjects to do his bidding but as desiring their free response in love.

This aspect of religion is to be observed particularly in the ethical life. Should one have the intention of carrying out a religious precept (*kavvanah*) before performing acts of good fellowship and human love? The teachers of the Lithuanian Mysar movement debated this question (Dov Katz, *Tenuat Ha-Musar*, vol. 5, Tel-Aviv, 1963, pp. 138–9). Rabbi Solomon Zalman Dolinsky used to recite the formula 'For the unification of the Holy One, blessed be He, and His Shekhinah (*leshem yihud*), before he performed an act of mercy. However, Rabbi Simhah Zussel of Kelm had a surer ethical touch when he argued that 'one should fulfil precepts of this kind out of natural feelings; they should stem the natural benevolence of a kind heart'. To invoke in this area the concept of a *mitzvah* is to frustrate the purpose of the command. Rabbi Sinhah Zissel gives an interesting turn to the verse: 'Love thy neighbour *as thyself*. Just as self-love is natural to man, requiring no calculations or special intentions, so should be his love for others. The man who has to have the intention of performing a *mitzvah* before he can love others will never progress beyond the I–It relationship, to use Buber's terminology, when what is required is the I–Thou. On the negative side, this ties up with Maimonides' famous analysis, in the sixth of his *Eight Chapters*, that with regard to ethical wrongdoing the better man is the one who has no need to exercise self-control in avoiding such things as theft and dishonesty but avoids them out of the goodness of his heart.

An apparently unpromising text for the relationship between religion and ethics is the verse: 'And Enoch walked with God' (Genesis 5:24). There is a Kabbalistic legend that Enoch was a cobbler, and when he stitched the upper part of the shoe to the lower he brought about unifications in the upper worlds. In its original form, this meant that Enoch was a contemplative recluse who did not think about the actual work he was doing but had his mind on the divine mysteries and thus promoted harmony between the upper and lower worlds, but the Musarists found such a notion ethically offensive. A cobbler with his mind on the Zohar instead of the work in hand will, in all probability, botch the job he is doing, be guilty of producing shoddy work, and gain money under false pretences. For this school the meaning is rather that by doing his job honestly and with integrity, by making good shoes, in his regard for his customers, Enoch served God and produced harmony in the upper worlds. (For this interpretation see Rabbi E. Dessler's *Mikhtav Me-Elijahu*, London, 1955, pp. 34–5.) Admirers of the Quaker family Cadbury used to boast that every tin of Bourneville cocoa manufactured by their firm was a good argument for religion. The question of a religious attitude towards vocation is of relevance here.

Prominent among theological topics which should receive treatment in the pulpit is the concept of revelation. Professor Manson of Manchester University used to tell how the renowned Biblical scholar, George Adam Smith, used to urge his pupils who were studying for the Christian ministry to avoid referring specifically to Biblical criticism in the pulpit even though they themselves should be thoroughly acquainted with the discipline. 'It is necessary to wash regularly,' he said, 'but one does not go out in public with soapsuds still on one's face.' This advice is still not without value if it is confined to the more technical aspects of critical theory. However, many of our people do have some idea of the tremendous strides modern Biblical scholarship has made and they wish to be instructed how to see the Bible in the light of the new knowledge. It can safely be assumed that the average congregant nowadays does not subscribe to the doctrine of verbal inspiration and recognizes that the Biblical books have to be seen against the background of the times in which they were written. Part of the preacher's task is to demonstrate how, none the less, these books stand out from the cultural environments in which they were written and whose vocabulary, literary style and even religous ideas they use; how, in the words of the famous epigram they are 'eternity expressing itself in time'.

Umberto Cassuto's work on the Pentateuch is far from being scholarship's final word on the subject, but is a happy hunting-ground for the preacher in this connection. Cassuto points out, for instance, that in nearly all ancient Near Eastern cosmologies there are unrelated monsters of chaos. The gods cannot begin to create until these monsters are destroyed. Cassuto connects these monsters with the *taninim* of Genesis 1:21. The author of Genesis (if we are talking of some acceptance of critical theory, it is permissible to use such a term) does not attack the old concept by direct assault but rejects it by implication. Far from God being unable to create until he destroys the pre-existing monsters, He creates the *taninim*. In this connection, Dr Hertz's comment on the Flood against this background is similarly helpful, though some of us would prefer not to treat the story of the Flood as factual.

Biblical passages such as that of the Flood should not be avoided in the pulpit. There is no harm at all, and occasionally much good, in repeating the note of catastrophe sounded in these passages: acorrupt world cannot survive. To preach otherwise in the name of what passes for Jewish optimism is a surrender to sentimentality, but this kind of thing should not be overdone. Thinkers who delight in telling us that God may wish to destroy His world are also not speaking with the voice of Judaism. Professor Suzuki, for instance, says (*Zen Buddhism*, New York, 1956, p. 275) that he cannot help being in deep sympathy with the Biblical writer who makes God soliloquize in this way: 'The Lord saw how great was man's wickedness on earth, and how every plan he devised was nothing but evil all the time. And the Lord regretted that He had made man on earth, and his heart was saddened. The Lord said: "I will blot out from the earth the men whom I have created – men together with beasts, creeping things, and birds of the sky, for I regret that I have made them"' Genesis (6:5–7). Suzuki continues: 'Is God now in earnest engaged in the gigantic task of effacing man from the earth? Apparently He is. If so, inasmuch as man is man, he must have a philosophy to cope with the situation. Can Zen offer this?' Whether or not Zen can offer this is another matter, but it is astonishing that Suzuki should have stopped short of the last verse in the passage he quotes: 'But Noah found favour with the Lord.' As Judaism sees it, there is always a Noah who makes the whole experiment worthwhile and introduces a new world and a new beginning. There is a middle road to be trodden between facile Victorian optimism and stark Buddhist pessimism.

In preaching on the theme of revelation it is essential to acknowledge frankly that once fundamentalism has been abandoned there are whole areas in which it is difficult to know where the word of God is to be found in the Bible. People do, indeed, find such an attitude irritating and expect certainty in the pulpit, protesting that the last thing they need is a doubting rabbi. The solution is for the Rabbi to point out that the search for Torah is itself Torah and as all the certainty of Torah. Long before the rise of any historical school, some of our great teachers expressed this idea. The Maharal of Prague, for instance, noted that the benediction before studying the Torah is: 'who has commanded us to busy ourselves with words of Torah' (*laasok be-divrey Torah*). We are not commanded to know whether Abbate or Rava is right in any absolute sense but rather to 'busy ourselves' in the words of both Abbaye and Rava, and this engagement is the Torah over which the benediction is recited. Helpful, too, in this connection is Mowinckell's examination of the Bible as 'the word of the Lord' (*dvar ha-shem*). He notes that *davar* means 'thing' as well as 'word'. The believer in verbal inspiration holds that in the Bible (for the Jew, the Bible as interpreted in the Rabbinic tradition) he is in possession of the *ipsissima verba* of the authors, indeed of God Himself. The more sophisticated believer cannot accept this notion for the soundest of reasons, but he, too, can find himself gripped by the divine 'thing', by the existential situation in which he struggles hard to discover what it is that God would have him do. He relives, as it were, in infinitely small measure, the experience of the prophets who were seized with an overwhelming conviction of complete commitment to the divine will. Rabbis should not allow themselves to be stampeded into dogmatism by the accusation of vagueness. To the objection that 'the fundamentalist lacks charity, the liberal clarity', they should retort, it is better to be vaguely right than definitely wrong.

A preacher should not be scared to introduce the idea of demythologizing. For instance, many thoughtful people, while acknowledging that the story of Adam and Eve is a myth, just do not know what to do with the story, how to understand it as relevant to their lives. The Rabbi can quote the famous Mishnah (*Sanhedrin* 4:5) on the reason why the human race is descended from one couple, that is, from Adam and Eve. This is to teach that whoever destroys a single life is considered as having destroyed a whole world, and whoever saves a single life is considered as having saved a whole world. Another reason is for the sake of peace, that no man should be able to say to his fellow: 'My father is greater than your father.' This is yet, another reason that the sectarians should not argue, as they would have done, that if many human beings were created originally, there are many gods. Finally, that God, unlike a human king, uses one seal and yet the 'coins' He stamps from it are all different. There is no doubt that the Rabbis who first expressed these opinions really did believe in Adam and Eve as historical figures, but in speaking as they did, they remind us of the true significance of the narrative and so make it as relevant for us as it was for them. It is not impossible that the particular emphases to which the Rabbis call attention were actually in the minds of those who told the story in the first place. This approach is valid for many other Biblical passages, the story of Jonah, for instance. Intelligent people now see that whether or not a big fish really can swallow a man is quite beside the point and fades into insignificance in relation to the living truth taught by this marvellous tale. It has rightly been said that the fish that swallowed Jonah was a red herring.

Many years ago a well-known, liberal Anglican vicar addressed the synagogue study group on the way he read Biblical stories of the kind mentioned. He gave the illustration of the Cinderella fairytale. Is the story true? If by this is meant, was there really a girl called Cinderella with a fairy godmother and a glass slipper that fitted only her foot, the answer is no. But if we mean do poor, neglected young girls with few prospects dream by the fireside of meeting the Prince Charming who will take them away from it all, the answer is yes.

One of the best ways of dealing with theological themes from the pulpit is to treat a good deal of theological language as symbolic, and to pursue the idea that much of Biblical language serves as a pointer to deeper significance. One way of considering Biblical symbols in this manner is the exploration of the good life as a way, a mountain or a ladder reaching from earth to heaven; the word of God as a tree, a hammer, a book, the sea, fire, water, milk, honey; the righteous as a cedar or a palm tree; man as dust and ashes. The Midrashic literature is full of rich spellings out of such Biblical symbols.

The symbol of the mountain ('who shall ascend the mountain of the Lord?') has great power even if the point is taken that it is an impersonal symbol. The distinguished mountain climber, Sir Arnold Lunn (*A Century of Mountaneering*, London, 1957, p. 15) has shown that the ancient Hebrews were the first to appreciate the beauty and strength of mountain scenery. The Greeks, for example, disliked mountains because, as Homer pointed out, they were useful only to bad men. The Hebrews did not accept utility as a criterion. The mystery and majesty of mountains were seen by the ancient Hebrews as a revelation of God's glory. Lunn is too

one-sided, but there is truth in what he says. Preaching on ascending the mountain of the Lord, the Rabbi can perhaps allude to
three aspects of mountain climbing. First, guides are essential for
the more difficult climbs. Judaism povides these in the great Jewish
teachers of the past. These, like all good guides, had a genius for
direction finding, but they had to proceed at first by trial and error;
because they worked hard to discover the best routes, they were
able to be of help to us as we endeavour to walk in safety in dangerous places. Second, every mountain climber knows the lure of
the summit. Rest is required periodically on the way up but the
peak always beckons. Jewish life, lived adventurously and by
means of stamina, is a constant striving towards a perfection that
can never be fully attained in this life. The Rabbis even say that the
disciples of the wise have real rest neither in this world nor in the
next. Third, some ascents are so demanding that they can be
attempted only by a team working together, as in the conquest of
Everest. Judaism places great stress on the community because
some of the most elevated spiritual insights are possible only when
the members of a group dedicated to their quest work together in
harmony and assist one another.

One example among many of Midrashic use of symbols is the
sermon Mekhiltta DRSBY to Exodus 19:18 (ed. Hoffman, p. 100) on
why the words of the Torah are compared to fire. Fire is life-giving
and the words of the Torah are life-giving. Fire must be
approached with caution. If a man keeps too far away from fire he
is frozen, but if he approaches too near he is in danger of being
scorched: a useful warning to religious enthusiasts to keep at a
suitable distance. Just as a small burning coal can help to kindle a
great bonfire, so the words of a 'little' man can set the soul of a
'great' man afire. And just as people whose daily work is connected with fire have a scorched appearance so, too, students of the
Torah are distinguished from others by their speech, their general
conduct and even by the way they dress.

No ingenuity is required to see how this Midrash can be developed into a full-scale theological sermon. The Torah has provided
the world with life-giving warmth and illumination and is still
capable of so doing. The Torah is so tremendous as a force that it
must be approached gradually and with care. Precisely because it
kindles man's heart and mind, he must ever be on his guard
against intolerance and fanaticism or a hazy, mindless overheating.
Furthermore, each person has his own way of looking at the Torah

and even a 'little' man can make his contribution. It is said that the Hafetz Hayyim would ask a little boy to tell him some Torah because, he said, every Jewish person has his (we would also say her) 'portion of the Torah' which no one but he can reveal. Finally, people who adhere find their whole being changed. They are, in the words of the Rabbis, 'children of the world to come'. Rabbi Yerucham Leibovitz, the Mashgiah of the Mir Yesshivah, used to say if an American or an Englishman or a Frenchman goes any-where in the world he betrays his origins by his mannerisms, his vocabulary, his accent and so forth. In the same way the person touched by the Torah is set apart by the vision he has seen. A soul that has been set alight by Sinai is never the same again.

Finally, a word might be said about the style of theological preaching. Here more than anywhere the rabbi must express his thoughts clearly. If he is uncertain about some aspects of the subject, as, indeed, he is bound to be, let him state quite clearly the reasons for his uncertainty. Solomon Schechter's remarks (*Studies in Judaism*, Philadelphia, 1945, vol. 1, p. 231) that 'the best theology is not consistent' has some force as a warning against facile solu-tions to the profoundest questions and as a reminder that we can-not fit the Deity into our tidy schemes. However, if it is taken as justification for loose and woolly thinking in the area of religion, it can lead all too easily to glorification of the absurd and a tacit admission that theology has nothing to do with truth. Holy non-sense is still nonsense; and in theological preaching, precisely because of the abstract nature of the subject, the pulpit language should be supple, energetic and intelligible, light and not too cate-gorical. The fatal temptation, as I know from experience, in writing and preaching on theological topics, is to camouflage precision with ponderous, solemn language in the mistaken belief that this alone is suitable to the seriousness and profundity of the theme. It is this attitude more than any other which has contributed to the hostility in which theology is held in some quarters.

There is a story told of Martin Buber. (When I repeated it years ago while proposing a vote of thanks to Buber he denied that it was true and said it was apocryphal.) It is said that soon after Buber had settled in Eretz Israel he was complimented on his Hebrew: 'Professor Buber, your Hebrew is excellent. I understand every word you say.' Buber is said to have replied that he would not be satisfied with his Hebrew until people would not be able to understand a word he said. For all the admiration for Buber's thought, it can hardly be denied that Buber is hard going. The old device in the language of sermons is particularly apt for thelogical preaching. Let the ideas you express be those of the most profound thinkers, but let the language you use to express them be that of the daily newspaper. The deeper the subject the greater should be the demand for clear, simple language. Or, as someone has said: you do not have to be fat in order to drive fat oxen.

PART TWO
GENESIS/*BERESHIT*

— 2 —

Bereshit

In the beginning… (Genesis 1:1)

This is the usual translation of *bereshit*, the very first word of the book of Genesis. Some Jewish commentators in the middle ages preferred the translation of this word as: 'In the beginning of', so that the verse means: 'When God began to create', hence the verse does not refer to the idea of a 'beginning' in the abstract. In any event the creation narrative in the book of Genesis remains silent on what was *before* the beginning. Modern scientific theories of the Big Bang lead to the scientifically unanswerable question: What was *there* before the Big Bang? To say that Time is itself a creation leaves completely obscure the whole idea of a time before Time was, of what was 'before' the before? Does it, in fact, make any sense to speak of a state outside Time? Some Jewish thinkers fall back on the idea that God created the world out of nothing. But 'nothing' is a term simply denoting a negation of everything else, not a 'thing' out of which something else can be made to appear. The solution adopted by the mystics is that everything there is came into being out of the Nothing that is God. God is called 'Nothing' in this context since of God as He is in Himself nothing can be said or even thought, so remote is this aspect of Deity from all human comprehension.

The human mind seeks always for a beginning without the quest ever being satisfied. With the philosopher Kant, we can either say that there never was a beginning, in which case an unimaginable idea is presented to the mind searching for a beginning. Or, we can say, there was a beginning and we are then obliged to persist in asking what was before that beginning. The same dilemma confronts us when we think of the end of everything. We cannot imagine a never-ending time and are still

compelled to ask whether this, too, has an end and become
involved in contradiction.

The same applies to Space. Is Space never-ending or is there a
limit to Space? However, the notion of an end to Space again
involves us in contradiction, in the idea of a 'space' outside or
beyond space, since, in the very postulation, we are thinking in
spatial terms. And is there any significance in the idea of eternity,
a state or stage beyond space or time? The poet Henry Vaughan
thought so when he wrote:

> *I saw Eternity the other night,*
> *Like a great ring of pure and endless light,*
> *All calm, as it was bright;*
> *And round beneath it, Time in hours, days, years,*
> *Driv'n by the spheres*
> *Like a vast shadow mov'd; in which the world*
> *And all her train were hurl'd.*

But Vaughan was a poet and the religious poets do try to imagine
the beyond and, when thinking about creation in a non-poetic
mode, the difficulties come crowding in.

When we think of the ancient myths, Assyrian and Babylonian
among others, in which the details of the 'before' and the gods are
given much prominence, we marvel at the silence of the Genesis
narrative, very much down to earth, a pure and magnificently simple statement implying: do not bother about the beyond. Even
when Genesis, followed by the rest of the Bible, speaks of God, it
is in terms of His relationship to man and his deeds. It is all in
terms of the here and now. Here is the arena in which the good
fight is to be fought, with the beyond left to God the Creator.

From the Jewish point of view, it is spiritually unhealthy for the
religious mind to dwell on the great mysteries that lie beyond
Creation while at the same time trying to live in the world which
has its origin in the transcendent. As the ancient Rabbis put it in
the Mishnah, compiled not later than the second century:

> The Creation narrative must not be expounded before two persons
> only before one [thus keeping the matter secret]. Whoever allows his
> mind to gaze at four things, it were better for him if he had not come
> into the world: what is above; what is below; what was behind; and
> what is in front. And whosoever takes no thought for the honour of his
> Creator, it were better for him if he had not come into the world.

These Rabbis were certainly not bent on curtailing speculation on the great mysteries, in which they themselves occasionally engaged. They do, however, issue a warning against hubris by which humans try to think of the unthinkable.

And he died ... (Genesis 5:5)

The striking resemblances between the early narratives of the book of Genesis and those in Assyrian and Babylonian sources makes it appear most probable that these early sources were utilized by the Biblical account, which, by purging them of their grosser elements and by reshaping them, made them suitable vehicles for the expression of moral and religious truths. By placing the two sets of narratives side by side, and noting how the Bible goes out of its way, so to speak, to reject the baser notions entertained in the ancient mythologies, we can see that the Hebrew Scriptures teach not only by what they include but also by what they omit.

Nowhere is this process more evident than in the antediluvian genealogy, with its fabulous life-span ascribed to the fathers of the generations from Adam to Noah. Granted that tales of heroes who lived far beyond the normal human span abound in ancient literatures, the prosaic account of men, who begat sons and daughters, lived for hundreds of years and then died, is something more than a bit of ancient mythology incorporated into Scripture.

In the literatures prior to or contemporaneous with the Bible, as Professor Cassuto noted long ago, the heroes who lived so long did so because they were not purely human but semi-divine beings, unaffected by the laws of growth and decay governing ordinary human life. The Bible tells this old story in its own way and so as to serve its own purpose, by making them all die before they had reached a thousand years – even Methuselah fails to live a complete 'day' of which the Psalmist says: 'A thousand years in Thy sight are but as yesterday when it is past' (Psalms 90:4). Furthermore, the attention of the reader of this genealogy is constantly drawn to human mortality by the oft-repeated refrain: 'And he died'.

It became typical of Judaism that man can be Godlike but he is not God. There exists an insurmountable barrier between the Deity and humans. '"For My thoughts are not your thoughts, neither are your ways My ways," saith the Lord'(Isaiah 55:8).

Recognition by humans of their insufficiency is the first step towards the acknowledgement of the need for reliance on God. It is the first move from a humanity futilely trying to exist by and for itself to a God-centred humanity, which worships Him as its Maker. All the rest of the Bible is a commentary to this tremendous idea.

And God said: 'Let there be light.' (Genesis 1:3)

Right at the beginning of the creation narrative, God creates light and, seeing that the light is good, makes a division between light and darkness. The idea of a conflict between spiritual light and darkness and the belief in the ultimate favourable outcome of the struggle, is a fundamental Jewish theme. The prophets, the psalmists and the sages all speak of their ideal in terms of light. Outside what might be called 'normative Judaism', the Dead Sea scrolls contain a vivid description of the battle between 'the sons of darkness' and 'the sons of light'.

Many of the Jewish rituals are connected with the kindling of lights. It is not so long ago since the pious felt honoured to present gifts of candles for the illumination of the synagogue. It is said that the famed Lithuanian saint, the Hafetz Hayyim, objected in his town to the wiring of his synagogue for electricity on the grounds that this would prevent people donating their individual gifts of candles. Although, nowadays, we do avail ourselves of the boon of electricity, in many synagogues candles are donated by individuals to burn on the reading desk and, late innovation though it is, synagogues everywhere have a perpetual light burning over the Ark.

Everyone wishes to see the victory of light over darkness. The difficulty is, however, that human beings rarely see matters in the stark terms of wholly dark or wholly light. Human vision is usually blurred, with the result that, in many of life's situations, there is no clear-cut division between right and wrong. In today's world, so many people of goodwill are arrayed against each other, each believing that he or she alone has seen the light and is in full possession of the truth.

The Talmudic Rabbis, commenting on the verse: 'Thou makest darkness, and it is night; wherein all the beasts of the forest do creep forth' (Psalms 104:20), remark that the verse speaks of this world of error, which is often enveloped in the darkness of night. The eighteenth-century moralist, Moshe Hayyim Luzzatto, with penetrating insight, notes that the comparison is not with total darkness, but with the confusing half light of night. At night, Luzzatto observes, we are not prevented from seeing anything at all, but we have a distorted vision, seeing a human being as a post or a post as a human being. Similarly, in human affairs, forces working openly for unmitigated evil are easily confronted and eventually defeated; their baseness and foulness stand out so blatantly that decent people are compelled to rise against them in anger, as they did when faced with Nazism, for example. It is when there is a blending of light and darkness – as in most of the difficult situations we are called upon to face – that we cannot see clearly where our duty lies and we tend to pass misleading and untrue judgements on those on the other side and, for that matter, on ourselves.

Is there a solution to this problem? Is it possible to break through the veil of obscurity that darkens counsel? There is no final solution, for such is the human predicament. Yet if we are to see the truth, we are obliged, so far as this is humanly possible, not to allow our moral judgements to be clouded by self-interest and personal desires. We have to try, at least, to to be honest with ourselves in assessing whether our judgements are guided, to use theological language, by the need to discover the will of God, which means, among other things, that we should not pronounce too readily that those on the other side belong to the sons of darkness with our side belonging triumphantly to the sons of light. As Oscar Wilde put it: the truth is rarely pure and never simple.

— 3 —

Noah

Noah was in his generation a man righteous and whole-hearted.   (Genesis 6:9)

Some of the ancient Rabbis, we are told, understood this verse to mean that Noah was a good man even in his corrupt generation; had he lived in the more righteous age of Abraham he would have been even more righteous. According to this interpretation, the goodness of Noah developed despite the dissolute age in which he lived, but he, like all men, was still influenced by his environment. Had Noah lived among good men, and not had to struggle against being tainted by the depravity of evil men, he would have risen far higher on the ladder of perfection. For his time Noah was a righteous man.

Another interpretation takes the verse to mean that Noah was a good man only *in relation to* his generation of evil men. In an age in which evil was triumphant, Noah's distinction consisted in the fact that, at least, he did not succumb to contemporary evil-doing. In the old story of the Rabbi who, desperate about having to deliver a eulogy over a man for whom he could find few redeeming features, asked around among the man's acquaintances, one of these said: 'Well, at least, he was better than his brother.' Had Abraham been one of Noah's contemporaries, Noah would not have stood out at all, compared with Abraham.

According to both the above interpretations goodness is a relative concept, so that in assessing whether or not a person is good do you look at those who are worse or those who are better? Even the less complimentary interpretation of the verse does not condemn Noah for not rising completely above the influences of his age, since it was into his age, and no other, that he was born for better or for worse. In Quiz shows a popular question is: 'If you could have been born into a different age, in which age would you choose to be born?' The fallacy in this kind of question is obvious. If 'you', with all your virtues and defects, were to live in another age, 'you' would not be the 'you' you are. You may admire the heroes of the past, but, even if it were possible for you to be transplanted among them, you can achieve this only by the other impossibility of losing your own identity. You can dream of being someone else, but such is an impossible dream, involving contradiction. There is no escaping our own identity, and to try to do so, whether in the mind or by imitation of others, is sheer folly.

With regard to Jewish communal life, for example, the temptation should be resisted of saying that Jewish life and loyalty were so much greater in former times. They may have been, though the past is often idealized, but even if they were we cannot reduplicate a past that has gone forever. Living in the present is the only valid course of action, though, naturally, we can and should be inspired by the good life of past generations. Medieval thinkers, who so stood in awe of ancient wise and good men that they felt totally insignificant, went on to maintain: Yes, we are only pygmies and the ancients were giants, but when a pygmy stands on a giant's shoulders his vision extends beyond that of the giant himself.

For the imagination of men's heart is evil from his youth.
(Genesis 8:1)

This verse – a key text in Christian theology for the doctrine of original sin – can serve, even in Jewish teaching, as a warning not to entertain an overoptimistic view of human nature. Human beings are not angels. To see it otherwise is to court frustration. Rousseau's bold declaration that mankind is intrinsically and naturally good received a terrible blow in the twentieth-century with its two world wars, with the Holocaust and with all the horrific massacres all over the brave new world of modernism.

There is much of value in the much more realistic assessment of post-modernism. 'Crisis theology' provided a salutary reminder of man's powerlessness to work out his own salvation. As the Biblical message constantly affirms, man needs God in his plight. Though the notion of original sin does not normally loom very large in Jewish teaching, except in the Kabbalah, there is still an emphasis on the way in which human deeds, lust for power, self-seeking motivation, together with a propensity for violence and hatred, can and frequently do lead to catastrophe. Modernism, which otherwise has so much to its credit, failed to acknowledge the darker side of human nature, often preferring to live in a fool's paradise.

Post-Modernism, unfortunately, tends to err in the opposite direction in order to favour a supposed realism that is itself utterly unrealistic. Some religious thinkers, nowadays, either postulate that man has 'come of age' and must learn to save himself, or else they despair of human betterment altogether. However, while, in some of the Psalms, for instance, there is a bitter cry to God 'out of the depths', there are to be found other Psalms in which gratitude is expressed for the enjoyment by man of long life and the fruits of his labours, naturally so since the true religious spirit accepts that God can be found not only where there is despair and intense suffering but also through human goodness, growth and success.

It should not be overlooked that our text, which speaks of the divine promise never again to bring a Deluge to destroy mankind, is basically more a message of hope than a severe warning. The verse implies that, while man must not delude himself into thinking that he is better than he really is, yet precisely because the imagination of his heart is evil from his youth, less is expected of him and God will help him when he recognizes his frailties. There is a lot to be said, from a religious point of view, for the implications of a well-known homily which takes the Hebrew *mineurav* to mean not 'from his youth' but rather 'because of his youth'. Human nature is evil because the human span on earth is very short without man having been given a lengthy period of trial and adaptation, education and improvement, growth and learning, struggle against evil and victory over it. If we think of, say, a year representing the age of the earth, then we must think of man coming on earth in only the last few minutes and civilization as evolving in only a few seconds. This is no more than an homiletical flourish but the idea behind it is sound. modernism is wrong in imagining that the victory has been won but post-modernism is also wrong in hinting that that the liberalism of modernism was bound to be a failure. As Franz Rosenzweig once said: 'It is all very well to attack the nineteenth-century but the nineteenth century was true.' The emergence of a more liberal attitude may have been a dream, but it is not a vain dream and can still be realized. It is certainly no nightmare. To be sure a religion like Judaism does not believe that man is capable of going it alone. But it does believe that, with God's help and inspiration, human progress is not an illusion but a living reality.

— 4 —

Lekh Lekha

Now the Lord said unto Abram: 'Get thee out of thy country, and from thy kindred, and from thy father's house'.
(Genesis 12:1)

The Hebrew, translated as 'Get thee', is *lekh lekha*, literally, 'Go to thyself'. The New English Bible simply renders the verse as: 'Leave your country', ignoring the two Hebrew words or, rather, treating them as an idiom for 'leaving'. Similarly, the Jewish Publication Society version translates the two words as 'Go forth'. The ArtScroll, following Rashi, translates as 'Go for yourself', that is, as Rashi expounds it in homiletical fashion, 'go for your own good', meaning, presumably, that God's command to Abram to leave his home and that of his father was not a tyrannical sheer test of obedience. It was, ultimately, for Abraham's benefit that he was told to go forth.

The Hasidic master, Yehudah Laib Alter, the Gerer Rebbe, author of the work *Sefat Emet*, gives a rather different, homiletical turn to the words *lekh lekha*, understanding them to mean: 'Go out to find yourself'. Before Abram could become, as the passage continues, a blessing to all the families of the earth, he had to find himself'; a surprisingly modern-sounding interpretation but true to the implications of the narrative. This is as if God is saying: no one, not even an Abram, can be of benefit to mankind, unless he first rids himself, to some extent at least, of the encumbrances of his family background, in Abram's case, of the idolatry practised by his father and the other polytheists of his time. The homily serves to point out the conflict in the souls of Abram's descendant, between particularism and universalism. In the narrative, too, Abram is given the name Abraham. A letter of the Tetragrammaton, the

letter *hey*, was added to the patriarch's original name, to denote, as
the Jewish tradition affirms, that Abraham's task was not only to be
himself the first great monotheist but to convert many others to the
true faith. To this day, a convert to Judaism is given the name
'son/daughter of our father Abraham'. Sarah, Abraham's wife, had a
hey added to her original name (Sarai) for the same reason. This is
made to explain the strange name of one of the ancient Rabbis, Ben
Hey Hey. It was conjectured that this Rabbi was a convert to
Judaism, hence he was known as the son of the patriarch and
matriarch, of Abraham and Sarah, the two who became father and
mother to all subsequent converts. All this is no more than pleasant
fancy unless it is appreciated that fanciful interpretation can be anything but whimsy when the deeper intent behind it is uncovered.

When urging the people he addressed to be faithful to the
teaching of their ancestor, Abraham, the prophet says:

> *Look unto Abraham your father,*
> *And unto Sarah that bore you:*
> *For when he was but one I called him,*
> *And I blessed him, and made him many.*
>   (Isaiah 51:2).

In this verse the prophet describes Abraham, a patriarch in
Christianity and Islam as well as in Judaism, as 'the one'. Just as
monotheism was unique in Abraham's day, the adherents of these
three religions have preferred to be loyal to Theism even when this
demanded a defiance of polytheism and idolatry. The ancient
Rabbis, again homiletical, understand the word *haivri* (the
Hebrew) used of Abraham, as if it came from the word *ever*, 'the
side'. He was called 'the one on the other side' because he was on
one side when everyone else in his time was on the other side.

This is the problem Jews have had to face when confronting
Western society. Judaism was still very different from other forms
of monotheism and Jews, in order to be true to their own vision,
were obliged to be on the other side even while being, so to speak,
on the same side in other important matters. They were obliged, as
the saying has it, to try to live in two civilizations. The ability
to uphold a truth firmly even when it is unpopular, the capacity for
independent thinking, for affirming that which many deny and to
deny that which others affirm, it is these qualities that have distinguished Judaism and made for the survival of the Jews. It has
rightly been said that the Jew is the eternal protestant.

The history of Judaism shows that there has been constant adaptation to other cultures where no firm matter of religious principle is involved. Jews in Hellenistic society wore Greek forms of dress and spoke Greek rather than Hebrew. Even the Torah – the Pentateuch – was translated into Greek and was read in Greek in the synagogue. In Persia, in Spain, in Arab lands, in Germany and in all the countries of the Diaspora, Jews copied many of the habits, the pattern of life, the fashions, even some of the beliefs and superstitions of their neighbours. The old saying has it that *wie es Christelt sich do Jidelt sich*. However, in matters of faith the Jew usually stood firm; in these matters he brooked no compromise. For these the Jew was prepared to make any sacrifice demanded of him.

There is a delightful story told of the great eighteenth-century teacher, Rabbi Jonathan Eybushitz, a man on friendly terms with the Christian clergy. A bishop, it is said, once protested to the Rabbi: 'You Jews disobey your own laws. According to Jewish law, if a piece of meat forbidden by Jewish law happens to get mixed with kosher meat the law is that if there are sixty times as much kosher meat in the dish the forbidden meat becomes neutralized – in the ratio of one to sixty – and the whole dish may be eaten. Since this is so,' the Bishop declared, 'and since there are more than sixty of us to the one of you, why do you persist in the refusal to become assimilated to us?' The Rabbi replied that the law of neutralization applies only where the piece of forbidden meat has lost its identity in the dish; but where it can be detected the piece of forbidden meat must be removed for the dish to be kosher. 'We Jews,' declared the Rabbi, 'do not lose sight of our true identity and in such cases the principle of neutralization never applies. We know why we exist, why we suffer and why we have to survive. It is not necessary to argue that the majority is always wrong to appreciate that the majority is often wrong. *Vox populi vox Dei* can serve as a useful guide in many of life's situations but has been rejected by Jews when it comes to the eternal verities.'

There is a test known to psychologists as the body-sway test. A person stands with his eyes closed and is subjected to repeated suggestions that he is falling. If, in spite of this, he remains in a fairly upright position, it can be assumed that he is emotionally mature; but if he gives way to the suggestion and falls, the chances are that he is immature. Jews, like other people, have not always been so secure in their faith that they never succumb to the hints or more than hints that their faith is false; but generally they have, like Abraham, withstood the test of religious maturity, natural to a religion that has been on the scene for some three thousand years, and, like Abraham, the Jew found that loyalty to his own became a blessing to 'all the families of the earth'. The Gerer Rebbe was anticipated by Shakespeare: 'This above all: to thine own self be true, and it must follow as the night the day, thou canst not then be false to any man.'

GENESIS 17:9–13.

Abraham is instructed to circumcise all his male descendants, just as he had been circumcised, as a sign of the covenant God had made with him and through him with them. Scripture offers no reason why this should be the particular sign of the covenant which, like other details of commands for which no reason is given, allows Jewish thinkers to suggest reasons in accordance with their particular philosophy of Judaism. A Midrashic passage is often quoted in this connection. It is said in this Midrash that Turnus Rufus, the Roman Governor of Palestine in the early second century, asked the great sage Rabbi Akiba the following question. 'If God dislikes a man having a foreskin, why did He create him with one?' A compelling, logical question from the Roman point of view; one that persisted in later Christian polemics against the rite of circumcision that Christianity had abandoned. Rabbi Akiba replies that God has created an incomplete world in order that human beings should have a role in bringing the world to perfection. The circumcision rite is thus seen as the removal by man of an appendage to his body for which there is no purpose except its removal as a symbol of total obedience to God's will. Naturally, this interpretation is particularistic since only the descendants of Abraham have to be circumcised, though the practice of circumcision was widespread among many peoples in ancient times.

The Rabbis of the Midrash were not systematic philosophers and their observation here is in the nature of a poetic homily. The medieval philosophers tried to deal with the question in a rationalistic way, especially the question of why the sign of the covenant should be expressed by the removal of the foreskin. Maimonides advances two reasons. The first is that circumcision weakens, without actually causing harm to, the organ of generation so that the sexual drives of the circumcised male are moderated. The bodily injury to that organ, says Maimonides, does not interrupt any vital function, nor does it destroy the power of generation, but it does counteract excessive lust. The second reason advanced by Maimonides is that the sign of the covenant had to be in that particular organ in order to prevent those who did not believe in pure monotheism claiming to be members of the covenantal people for reasons of their own. The operation is so difficult and so disagreeable that no one would undergo it unless he sincerely wished to belong to the people of faith. Philo of Alexandria was the first to advance the hygienic reason. The foreskin is literally unclean and can be a source of disease. The more usual reason advanced by Jewish thinkers is the obvious one that the sign of the covenant throughout all generations has to be in the very organ of generation. Whatever the original reason, faithful Jews throughout the ages have circumcised their male children as the most distinctive sign of their loyalty to God.

Va-yerah

In the Hagar story we read how Abraham was told by God to send his concubine and her child away from his tent and how, straying in the wilderness without water, she cast the child away from her, sitting without hope to await his death 'a good way off, as it were a bowshot' (Genesis 21:16).

The story goes on to tell how God had compassion on the child and saved him from death, and it concludes with the words: 'And God was with the lad and he grew; and he dwelt in the wilderness, and became a wielder of the bow.' It can hardly be simply a coincidence that the word 'bow' occurs twice, once at the beginning of the narrative, when the child had been cast away, at a distance of a *bowshot*, and once again at the end of the narrative when the lad whose life had been spared grew up to be a wielder of the *bow*. With its usual economy of words, Scripture appears to suggest that there is a causal connection between the image of the bow in Hagar's mind when she cast the child away and the fact that when the lad grew up he became a wielder of the bow. In moments of severe crisis even the most sophisticated and the most civilized is often tempted against his will to cast off his restraints and to revert to his primitive ancestor the caveman. This is exemplified in our story.

We are told very little about Hagar's background. According to a rabbinic tradition attempting to fill the gaps, Hagar was an Egyptian princess who had forsaken the glory of her father's court in order to cast in her lot with Abraham, the teacher of God's mercy and compassion. Be that as it may, she was certainly of pagan origin, a brave woman in whose memory there still abided the boast of her people's prowess with the bow, the symbol of sport but also of fierce battles and the hunt for prey. In Abraham's tent she had no doubt preferred other, less savage symbols. Yet in that tremendous crisis in her life, when her child was helpless, it was the image of the bow, the most potent image she still possessed deep down in her heart, that sprang to her mind. Hagar, the daughter of a war-loving, violent people, as she removes herself in bitter despair from her dying child, measures her distance by the shot of the bow. It is not surprising, the narrative implies, that when the child grew up the bow was for him the most potent of symbols and he became a bowman.

Modern psychology has made us familiar with the fuller meaning of the saying that the child is father to the man. The most formative years, we now know, are the childhood years. Character is shaped in infancy. What a fine and penetrating comment on Jewish teachings regarding the significance of home life on a child's character and the importance of training in the good life during the early years. We can now appreciate, perhaps to a greater degree than our ancestors, the wisdom of all the lovely ceremonies that have as their aim the introduction of the child at a tender age to the sweetness and light of the Torah. For, as the Rabbis say, the speech of a child in the street is but an echo of that of its parents in the home.

The Hagar story reminds us that our lives will influence our children whether we like it or not. It reminds us of the folly of pretending that we can be indifferent to Jewish values and yet leave our children supposedly free to make up their own minds about Judaism when they grow up. For, in being the kind of parents we are, we make the choice for our children as well as for themselves. As the Deuteronomist says: *'therefore choose life, that thou mayest live, thou and thy seed'*.

GENESIS 22

This chapter, in which is told how Abraham is instructed by God to take his son Isaac to Mount Moriah and offer him up as a burnt offering, is known in the Jewish tradition as the *Akedah*, the 'binding' (of Isaac on the altar). The *Akedah* has been a dominant feature of Jewish religious thought from the third century at least, though there is some evidence that it was not so prominent before that period. In the middle ages the *Akedah* became the supreme symbol of Jewish martyrdom for the faith.

The tremendous problem with regard to the *Akedah* is the idea that God should command a father to sacrifice his son. Everywhere else in the Bible child sacrifice is totally abhorrent. Arising out of the initial problem are further questions regarding Abraham's intention to carry out the terrible deed. How could Abraham have been so sure that God had, indeed, ordered him to kill his innocent child? Even if he was convinced that God had so commanded him, was it his duty to obey? Is obedience to God's will so supreme an obligation that it can override man's moral sense, demanding of him that he commit a criminal act of the worst kind for the glory of God? Can or should one worship a being who wishes to be served by an act of murder? Moreover the very God who commanded the sacrifice of Isaac had himself performed the miracle of giving Isaac to Abraham and Sarah when they were of advanced age and had promised Abraham that, through Isaac, Sarah would be a mother of nations (Genesis 17:15–19; 18:10–15; and 21:1–12).

Three different attitudes to the problem have been adopted by Jewish thinkers. The first stresses the story's 'happy ending'. Abraham is, in fact, eventually commanded not to slay his son, to 'stay his hand'. On this view the whole episode was only a 'test', a divine vindication of Abraham's absolute trust in God. There never was a divine intention for Abraham to kill Isaac. God, being God, could never so deny His own nature, so to speak, as to wish a man to commit murder out of obedience to Him. The second attitude stresses, on the contrary, the original command. This view, very close to Kierkegaard's attitude, can imagine God commanding Abraham to slay his son. True, the order is revoked at the last moment, but the point has been made, none the less, that, in Kierkegaard's terminology, there can be, so far as the 'knight of faith' is concerned, a 'teleological suspension of the ethical'. Abraham goes in 'fear and trembling' (in the title of Kierkegaard's notable book on the subject) but the ultimate for him is not the ethical norm but his individual relationship to his God. A third attitude seeks to dwell on both aspects of the narrative. On this view, it is impossible that God could ever, in reality, be false to His own nature and command an act of murder, and yet, *if* He could, then, indeed, Abraham would have been obliged to cross the fearful abyss. It must be said that these three attitudes are rarely given sharply defined expression in the Jewish sources. They tend to blend into one another, and among some of the Jewish thinkers all three are combined without any awareness that a contradiction is involved. It is thus more a matter of where the emphasis is placed than of precise categorization. It can be argued that, after all, the story, as we now have it, does consist of these two parts, the original command and the 'happy ending', that this is the only occasion on which God is said to have commanded a man to commit murder as a test of obedience; that, on the other hand, to read the story as simply a homily on the sanctity of human life is to reduce it to banality; and, at the same time, to overlook the finale is to ignore an element that the narrator never intended should be overlooked. For these reasons, some modern thinkers, especially, have tried to preserve both elements as essential to the *Akedah*.

A passage in the Talmud (tractate *Sanhedrin* 89b) on the *Akedah* deserves to be quoted in full as evidence of the way the ancient Rabbis saw the tensions in the narrative:

> *And it came to pass after these words that God did tempt Abraham* [Genesis 22:1]. What is the meaning of *after*? Rabbi Johanan said in the name of Rabbi Jose ben Zimra: *After* the words of Satan, it is written: *And the child grew up and was weaned and Abraham made a great feast the same day that Isaac was weaned* [Genesis 21: 8]. Satan said to the Holy One, blessed be He: Sovereign of the Universe! Thou didst give a son to this old man at the age of a hundred, yet of all the banquet he prepared he did not sacrifice to Thee a single turtle-dove or pigeon! God replied: Did he not do all this in honour of his son! Yet were I to tell him to sacrifice that son to Me he would do so at once … On the way [as Abraham was leading Isaac to be slaughtered] Satan confronted him and said to him: *If we assay to commune with thee, wilt thou be grieved?...Behold. thou hast instructed many, and thou hast strengthened the weak hands. Thy words have upholden him that was falling, and thou hast strengthened the feeble knees. But now it is come upon thee, and thou faintest* [Job 4: 2–5,i.e. Abraham is being asked to commit a wrong against which his whole teaching had been directed]. Abraham replied: *I will walk in my integrity* [Psalms 26:2]. Satan said to him: *Should not thy fear be thy confidence* [Job 4:6]. He replied: *Remember, I pray thee, whoever perished being innocent?* [Job 4:6]. Seeing that Abraham would not listen to him, Satan said to him: *Now a thing was secretly brought to me* [Job 4:12]: I have heard from behind the Veil *the lamb, for a burnt offering* [Genesis 22: 7] but not Isaac for a burnt offering, Abraham replied: It is the punishment of a liar that he is not believed even when he tells the truth.
>
> In the parallel passage in the Midrash (Genesis Rabbah 56:4) Satan says to Abraham: 'Tomorrow He will condemn thee as a murderer,' to which Abraham retorts: 'Nevertheless!'

The command to Abraham was, on any showing, a once-and-for-all matter, never to be repeated and actually not carried out even in the instance of Abraham himself. Yet this does not allow a Jewish thinker to dismiss the Kierkegaardian 'Midrash' as utter nonsense. There is point in the reminder that a true religious outlook demands of 'ethical man' that he acquire a vertical direction to his life and that when the brave 'knight of faith' goes out to do battle he does not tilt at windmills.

Hayye Sarah

Abraham was now old, advanced in years. (Genesis 24:1)

A fine Rabbinic comment on this verse notes that the Hebrew words *ba bayamim*, translated as 'advanced in years', can mean 'advanced in days', otherwise it is obvious that if Abraham was old he must have been 'advanced in years'. However the expression 'advanced in days' can have the meaning that Abraham 'advanced' day by day. He made the most of every day in his service of God. His life was not static but of a constant growth in the understanding of his role. Some people grow old without really growing up.

> *I will make you swear by the Lord, the God of heaven and the God of the earth, that you will not take a wife for my son from the daughters of the Canaanites among whom I dwell.*
>
> (Genesis 24:3)

For the Rabbis of the Midrash, every word and even every letter of the Torah was written with a purpose. For them, important lessons could be derived not only from the great passages of the Torah or from whole verses but even from individual words and letters. Students of classical Hebrew know that in the Bible certain words are written with their full quota of vowel letters while these vowel letters are sometimes omitted even in the same word. For the Rabbis there was nothing arbitrary about this. They noted that when the vowel letters are left out the word can change its meaning. The variant meaning can then be seen as a hint that there is another meaning besides that which appears on the surface. It is true that scholars today understand the different way of spelling the word as due simply to scribal whim; but, the Rabbis would say, there is room for a good homily where one can find it.

A good example of the Rabbinic method is found in a comment on the story of Abraham sending his faithful servant, Eliezer, to bring back a young woman as a suitable wife for Isaac, Abraham's son. The servant is sent for this purpose to the home of Abraham's kinsman. The servant, described as 'the oldest servant in his household, the man who took charge of all he had', is prepared to go on his mission but before he sets out he objects: 'Suppose the woman is unwilling to follow me to this land...?' The dialogue between Abraham and his servant is reported by the servant when he describes the event after Rebekah had been chosen. Thus we find two accounts of the dialogue: one when the servant is about to set out and another when the servant tells the tale. Now the Midrash notes that in one account the Hebrew word for 'suppose', *ulai*, is written in full, with the vowel letter *vav*. But in the other account it is written without the *vav* and can be read as *elai*, meaning 'to me'. The explanation of the change is that Eliezer had a daughter of his own and he had the ambition deep in his heart for Isaac to marry her. When Eliezer said, 'Suppose the woman is unwilling [to come back with him]', then his mission would fail; he had the secret wish that she would come 'to me', that is, his daughter would become Isaac's wife. As a faithful servant Eliezer wanted to do the will of his master but, deep down, there was the hidden hope that the mission would be a failure. He must have known that had it been his master's intention for Isaac to marry his daughter, his master would not have sent him to find a wife for Isaac at the home of his kinsman. As a faithful servant, Eliezer intended to carry out Abraham's instructions to the letter in order to bring the matter to a conclusion that would be in conflict with his own deepest interests. However, personal bias is not so easily disregarded. The Midrash invents a new character, Eliezer's daughter. The Rabbis of the Midrash probe acutely Eliezer's mind and suggest that determined though he was to carry out Abraham's wishes he could not really stifle the hope that the woman will be unwilling to come back with him so that Isaac will then be forced to marry his own daughter. Eliezer's forlorn hope was for a different 'happy ending'.

This Midrashic comment is more than a fanciful play of words. The Midrashic Rabbis were keen students of the human mind.

What they had to say about the servant of Abraham is relevant beyond the immediate context. For in every one of life's situations there is an element of self-interest conflicting with the wider interests we are obliged and want to pursue; and self-interest is often in itself a call of duty and for worthy ends. Eliezer wanted his daughter to marry Isaac out of the most laudable of motives. After all, he must have said to himself, who were better qualified to carry forward Abraham's teaching than Abraham's servant and his daughter who are so close to him? Even when it becomes clear on the surface that the wider interest must take precedence, it is hard to still the voice within that cries: 'To me'.

Some thinkers go so far as to suggest that human beings can never really eradicate feelings of self-interest. On this view even when humans perform the most altruistic of acts they think, consciously or unconsciously, of what they themselves are going to get out of it. It is not necessary to agree with these thinkers to appreciate that the old Jewish teaching of acting 'for the sake of Heaven' is an ideal, one capable of being fully realized by only the greatest of saints and even for these only occasionally. This is why the Talmudic Rabbis teach that humans should persevere in living the good life even when the motive for so doing is tainted by self-interest. For, say the Rabbis, out of the self-seeking motivation the purer motivation will follow. This does not mean that the self-seeker will suddenly wake up one morning to find himself completely altruistic. Human nature does not change overnight and realism is also a virtue. What it does mean is that, whatever the original motivation for a man to embark on the good way, that man can become so engrossed in the pursuit of the good that, in the process, he forgets himself sufficiently to follow the truth for its own sake.

Take, for instance, the man who accepts a position of trust in the community because he believes he will gain kudos from it. True, he thinks primarily of his own honour, but when he engages in his task he forgets all about what he personally stands to gain and enjoys working for the community as a good servant. Doing things 'for the sake of Heaven' is never a position that can be held permanently but one to which we can only hope to approximate. A realistic religious attitude in this matter is to carry on regardless while still offering the prayer of the ancient Jewish prayer: 'Purify our hearts to serve Thee in truth.'

— 7 —

Toledot

And Jacob was a quiet man, dwelling in tents. (Genesis 25:27)

The patriarch Jacob is described as a 'quiet man', *ish tam* in the Hebrew; the AV renders this as 'a plain man'; the New Jewish translation as 'a mild man'; Skinner translates it as 'an orderly man'. The meaning seems to be that, unlike Esau, his brother, the hunter, the 'man of the field', Jacob led a quiet, simple life. He dwelt in tents.

On the face of it, this characterization of the two brothers and rivals does not seem to square with the facts given in the rest of the narrative. As the story continues Esau appears as the man of more simple and uncomplicated character. Esau is wild, free, generous, impulsive, easily moved, responsive to his surroundings. He is a man of immediate passions and acute emotions. Jacob, on the other hand, is the tortured wrestler with himself and with others. He is the man capable of tricking his brother and yet he can dream of the ladder reaching to the heavens with the angels ascending and descending. In the psychological jargon of our day, Esau is healthily outgoing by nature, an extrovert, while Jacob is all introspection and inner conflict, an introvert if ever there was one.

It is now widely recognized that in the Patriarchal narratives we have not only stories about individuals but descriptions of national characteristics. Jacob and Esau, for example, are made to represent the different attitudes towards life of the rival nations, respectively of the nations Israel and Edom. The distinguished American Jewish scholar, H. L. Ginzberg, is reported to have said that one of the ways of understanding Genesis is to see the Patriarchs rather like the way the Americans see the figure of Uncle

Sam and Englishmen John Bull. Into these figures Americans and Englishmen read those ideas and ideals they consider to be typical of their national distinctiveness. The Israelites must have appreciated that in some way the Edomites were superior to the people of Israel. However, they also saw that in Israel a great new idea was emerging, the idea that God had a task for them to perform, a task that was ultimately to bring God to the whole world, and in this idea lay the justification for their own existence. This is what they meant when they spoke of Esau, the progenitor of Edom, as a skilful hunter, and of Jacob, the ancestor of their own people, as a 'quiet man'. They probably meant that for all their lack of proficiency in other matters, the people of Israel were prepared to be dominated or, perhaps one should say, came to be dominated, by a great idea with all the suffering involved in the struggle. It is not going too far from the plain meaning of *ish tam* to translate this as 'a man of ideas', even though, given the concrete nature of classical Hebrew, the notion of an 'idea' in the abstract is foreign to this language and those who used it.

It is commonly held that the ideas man is impractical. He is often thought of as an unworldly dreamer, remote from material concerns, clumsy with his hands, all thumbs, the very embodiment of an absented-minded professor. The usual defence is the retort that even though this is a caricature it might none the less have some truth, and yet ideas have value and must be preserved, so that it is necessary to tolerate the ideas man for the sake of his ideas and simply put up with his eccentricities. Such is, however, a poor and inadequate defence.

The truth is rather that it is ideas that change the world; that it is theory which results in the most decisive forms of action; that there is nothing more practical than intellectual perception. When all is said and done, it was not the world-conquerors who transformed the world but the thinkers, the poets, the sages and the prophets. Alexander the Great and Julius Caesar are figures in the history books but the writings of Plato and Aristotle are still studied all over the world and continue to exert their influence. Fosdick rightly observed that Nebuchadnezzar, the mighty ruler before whom kings trembled, is known today chiefly as the king in whose reign the prophet Jeremiah prophesied. Those responsible for most of the action in human history were not themselves primarily men of action but men of ideas – the Hebrew prophets, Homer, Jesus, Mohammed, Aquinas, Shakespeare, Newton,

Darwin, Freud, Einstein. Not that all the ideas of all these men were beneficial. Some of their ideas have been pernicious. But that they have been of tremendous power in human affairs cannot be denied. In the words of Arthur William Edgar O'Shaughnessy:

> We are the music-makers
> And we are the dreamers of dreams,
> Wandering by lone sea-breakers,
> And sitting by desolate streams;
> World-losers and world-forsakers
> On whom the pale moon gleams:
> Yet we are the movers and shakers
> Of the world for ever, it seems.

— 8 —

Vayetzey

And he dreamed, and behold a ladder set up on the earth,
and the top of it reached to heaven; and behold the angels
of God ascending and descending on it. (Genesis 28:12)

Jacob's dream of the ladder reaching to heaven, with the angels of God ascending and descending on it, has captured the imagination of commentators throughout the ages. The account has invited so many different interpretations and adaptation to the religious life that to try to say something new is futile. Here are offered one or two observations based on Jewish sources.

First to be noted is the expression used of the angels. They ascend and descend. Since the angels live, so to speak, 'up there', we would have expected the verse to say 'descending' before 'ascending'. The angels presumably had first to come down before they went up again. The answer according to the plain meaning is that people normally describe a movement from above to below and from below to above as 'up and down', as we do in English, and this idiom is adopted even when, as in this instance, the first movement is from above to below.

Preachers, however, are not interested in the plain meaning of a verse when they can give it a pleasing, though fanciful turn if the result is captivating. Thus a Midrashic interpretation has it that two groups of angels are referred to, those who had accompanied Jacob in the Holy Land and those who were to accompany him outside the Holy Land. The former, having accomplished their mission, went up first to their abode in heaven and then the latter came down in order to carry out the tougher mission of protecting Jacob in a more hostile environment. This is as if to say that the harder and more risky the role God gives to each individual, the greater the protection from harm is given to him by God. A further interpretation is offered. God's mercy, even when it extends to spiritual matters, can only operate fully if human goodwill is first sent on high to enable the divine grace to flow. As the Kabbalists are fond of putting it: 'The impulse from below bestirs the impulse from on high.'

THE THREE THINGS THE LADDER IS MADE TO REPRESENT

Jewish preachers in the middle ages often used Gematria to make their point. The term Gematria comes from the Greek and resembles our word geometry. The method is far-fetched but can often be used to convey important truths or, better, as a reminder of important truths. The method is based on the fact that each letter of the Hebrew alphabet is also a number:, e.g. *alef*, the first letter, is one; *bet*, the second letter, two and so on.

A good example of this is the way the word for 'ladder' (*sulam*) is treated. The Gematria (numerical value) of *sulam* is the same as that of three other words - *kol, tzom* and *mamon* - each having the numerical value of 136.The word *kol* means 'voice', the word *tzom* means 'fasting' and the word *mamon* means, of course, money or wealth. These three things each form a ladder with its feet on the ground and its head in the heavens; consequently, though they belong to the material world, they can become of spiritual import.

The human 'voice', when used to denigrate others or in false propaganda, is so often a source of evil. But when used in prayer and worship it reaches to the heavens. 'Fasting' or asceticism in general is not necessarily a religious activity. Ascetics can become heartless; hard on themselves, they can easily be tempted to score over others or be harsh in their treatment of those they consider to be inferior mortals without moral stamina. However, there is still high value in the kind of asceticism which prevents human beings becoming too absorbed in worldly things to the detriment of the spiritual life. Similarly, the acquisition of wealth can result in pride, the pursuit of power and sheer dishonesty. Yet wealth can be a source of good when it is obtained honestly and used for the benefit of society.

So far as Judaism is concerned, communications – in our day, especially, the media – are neutral. They are neither good nor bad in themselves. It all depends on why and how they are used.

Self-denial is similarly neutral, depending on its operation; and wealth, too, is neutral in itself. What matters is the way it is earned and employed.

> *And it came to pass, when Laban heard the tidings of Jacob his sister's son, that he ran to meet him, and embraced him, and kissed him, and brought him to his house.*
> (Genesis 29:13)

The Hebrew word *shema* translated as 'tidings' is the word used in the Book of Esther to describe the 'fame' of Mordecai, that is,Mordecai's reputation. The verse expresses the thought that only when Laban heard of the fame and prowess of his nephew did he run to welcome him to his house. It was only when Laban came to realize that Jacob was a useful person to have around, that he thought it a good idea to welcome such potential, from which he himself might benefit.

In an earlier portion of Genesis we meet with Laban and here, too, his grasping nature is subtly delineated with a stroke of the pen:

> *And it came to pass, when he saw the ring, and the bracelets upon his sister's hands, and when he heard the words of Rebekah his sister saying: 'Thus spoke the man unto me', that he came unto the man.* (Genesis 24: 30)

Laban is not eager to offer hospitality and welcome to the tired and hungry wayfarer, even though he was his kith and kin. Nor does Laban share any of the concern for the plight of the weary and thirsty traveller shown by his sister Rebekah. It is only when he sees the rings and the bracelets, the promise of wealth and prosperity, and realizes that he is on to a good thing that he runs to welcome his guest. And, years later, Laban, now a father and a man of substance and position, is still not cured of his rapacity. The fact that his own nephew is in dire need means nothing to him. Only when he hears of Jacob's fame, when he hears of his great strength in rolling the boulder from the well single-handed, does Laban run to invite Jacob to become a member of the family. Jacob, Laban thinks, will be a very capable farmhand and, moreover, Laban has two daughters to marry off.

Laban is the opportunist *par excellence*, the man with his eye always on the main chance. He is the supreme example of the man who approaches every situation with the thought: 'What's in it for me?' Expediency is the guiding principle of the opportunist, whereas the truly sympathetic man sees others as persons in their own right, even though he, too, cannot escape entirely from an element of self-interest. The opportunist, even when he affords help and assistance to others, sees them as tools to be used for his own ends.

There is a verse in the Book of Daniel – a famous non-Jewish preacher described it as the greatest text in the Bible – which affords a glimpse into the character of men whose lives were a direct antithesis to all that a Laban stands for. In the well-known story of Shadrach, Meshach and Abed-nego, who refused to bow to the great king's idol and were prepared to be cast into the furnace for their faith, we hear of their defiant challenge. They exclaim that God can save them if He so wills, and they trust that He will do so. They go on to say: 'But, if not, let it be known unto thee, O king, that we will not serve thy gods, nor worship the golden image thou hast set up' (Daniel 3:18). Here we have three youths of noble character who are prepared not only to live but if needs be to die for their faith. If God will save them, they declare, well and good. *But if not* ... they will still remain loyal to their principles even unto death.

The question of martyrdom is complicated. Judaism does not encourage the willing pursuit of martyrdom. Yet when it does come, as it did in ancient and medieval times, Jews saw themselves obliged to give all in the name of their religion. There can certainly be no doubt about Judaism's attitude to opportunism. Every person can be a person of stern unbending principle like the three youths or a person of base expediency like Laban. There can be no doubt which of the two types evokes admiration. In the Jewish tradition, Laban is almost a figure of fun. For all his plotting and scheming to feather his own nest, he somehow always seems to come off worse in the end. It is as if the tradition wishes to underscore the truth that the man who goes through life with the sole aim of benefiting himself is soon found out. He not only lives a useless life, without really being of service to anyone else, but, in the final analysis, he does not find happiness for himself.

— 9 —

Va-yishlah

And Jacob sent messengers before him to Esau his brother.
(Genesis 32:4)

On this verse Rashi comments in the name of the Midrash: 'real *malakhim*'. That is to say, although the word *malakh*, 'messenger', can mean anyone sent to perform a task, in the Bible the word usually denotes a heavenly messenger, an angel. (Compare the etymology of the English word 'angel'.) Thus, while according to the plain meaning Jacob might be imagined to have sent purely human messengers, and this is the conventional rendering in English translations, Rashi says that Jacob sent 'real *malakhim*', namely, not mere human messengers but heavenly angels.

Rashi's comment is not as fanciful as it seems on the surface but is very close to the plain meaning of the narrative since the previous two verses clearly refer to the 'angels of God' who met Jacob as he went on his way (and there occurs, at the beginning of the previous *sidra*, the dream of Jacob in which he saw the angels on the ladder reaching heavenward). Since, Rashi implies, Scripture has told us that Jacob had been visited by a company of angels, and, immediately afterwards, we are told that he sent *malakhim* (the same word being used in both instances) the reference is presumably (so evidently Rashi and the Midrash argue) to the same visitors from on high.

And yet the verse does not say that Jacob sent *ha-malakhim*, 'the angels', as it would have done were the reference to the angels mentioned in the earlier verse. It is possible that, in fact, Scripture is intentionally ambiguous on whether earthly or celestial beings are involved as the Patriarch's destiny unfolds.

Later on in the *sidra*, a mysterious being comes at night to wrestle with Jacob. From various indications as the narrative proceeds it becomes clear that this is no ordinary assailant, but one sent from on high; yet, the verse states, he arrives on the scene as a 'man'. According to Maimonides, angels are spiritual forces which human beings can see in corporeal form only in dreams. According to the Zohar, on the other hand, the angels are spiritual forces so far above the material world that if they are to appear to humans they must adopt the garments of this world and appear not only in dreams but also actually appear, albeit in corporeal form.

The whole question of the existence of angels is very complex. Some of the medieval teachers, such as Rashi, preferred to stress whenever they could that there are real supernatural beings called angels who are sent to do God's will, though they admit that named angels such as Michael and Gabriel, found only in late Biblical passages, are different from the generic form found in the earlier Biblical texts. Indeed, the Talmudic Rabbis say that the names of particular angels were brought to the Jews by the people who came from Babylon.

The ancients, even when they did not actually see the angels, could dream of seeing them and, in the process, really did see them. Our *sidra* is a reminder that the mundane world is not too infrequently invaded by the spiritual and that, for those who have eyes to see, quite ordinary messengers are, as Rashi says, 'real *malakhim*'.

And Jacob was left alone… (Genesis 31:25)

Jacob wrestled with the angel when he was 'left alone'. Dr Hertz's commentary quotes with approval the words of Dean Stanley:

> This mysterious encounter of the Patriarch has become the universal allegory of the struggles and wrestlings on the eve of some dreadful crisis, in the solitude and darkness of some overhanging trial.

The Rabbis of the Midrash noted that the Hebrew word *levado* – meaning 'alone' – is used here of Jacob and the same word is used of God in Isaiah's prophetic vision concerning the end of days: 'And the Lord alone [*levado*] shall be exalted in that day' (Isaiah 2:11).

Loneliness can be a terrible curse. Few human beings are more to be pitied than the person without any friends or companions and obliged to take his pilgrimage alone. This is one of the great social problems to be endured in a great city like London. What a terrible thought it is that there are people in the great metropolis who are fated to move about in the crowds of their fellows indifferent to their hopes and fears, indifferent, indeed, to their very existence. How could people live at all if it were not through the realization that their anxieties are shared by others, that human beings can sustain and support one another like hungry and cold little children huddling together for warmth. In the well-known Talmudic legend of Honi the Circle Drawer, this saint went to sleep for seventy years. When he awoke to find all his old companions long dead, he went on to pray that God should allow him to die since, he said, he wanted either friends or death. In the Creation narrative at the beginning of the Book of Genesis, before God creates Eve, he says of Adam that it is not good for 'the man to be alone' (*levado*, used once again).

There is, however, an aspect of loneliness that is not only unavoidable but of the greatest value – the loneliness of man in the presence of God. Whitehead's definition of religion as 'what a man does with his solitariness' is too narrow so far as Judaism is concerned – after all the social obligations are also *mitzvot*, precepts of the Torah, and hence just as much religious as prayer for example – yet Whitehead is right that an important aspect of the religious life is for the soul to be alone with its Creator. When we wrestle with life's problems, when we are called upon to make some agonizing decision, we can be helped and encouraged and even advised by those we love and by others as well, but in the final analysis, we have to fight it out for and in ourselves. Jacob is alone when he wrestles with the angel and yet he is with God, of whom the word 'alone' is also used.

The word *levado* can mean 'unique' as well as 'alone'. It is used in the former sense in the verse from Isaiah which speaks of God being *levado* on that day. Herein lies a great truth. In a sense we are all bound to face life alone because each individual is unique. There are bound to be some experiences and attitudes that must remain our own, not to be shared with others who are also unique individuals. In the Talmud it is said that God used the copy of Adam, the first man, to mint the coins of all Adam's descendants. Yet, though all from the same mould, no two human beings are exactly alike, differing, as the rabbis put it, in their minds as they differ in their features (we would today say in their fingerprints and in their genes). In each individual there is a fraction of God's truth that only he or she can reveal.

What else but this is exhibited by the long history of the Jewish people, that Jews have a way of life, that they have in their possession truths about God and His relationship to man, that they cherish ideals of value to themselves and which, ultimately, will become the common property of all mankind. Jews have been pre- pared to 'live in a corner', as a critic once said. Jews have been ready to live in isolation when needs must, painful though it has been and, to some extent, still is. Jewish separateness, at its best, has not been a matter of seclusion for its own sake but a means of preserving the most precious thing of all, the Jewish people's covenant with God. Jacob will continue to be alone until the day comes when the God of Jacob will be acknowledged by the whole of mankind. When that day comes the Lord alone will reign and Jacob will be alone no more.

> *And Jacob came to Shalem, a city of Shechem, which is in*
> *the land of Canaan, when he came from Paddan-aram; and*
> *encamped before the city.*   (Genesis 33:18)

The Midrashic interpretation of the word *shalem* is not as a place- name, but in its literal meaning of 'whole'. Jacob, says the Midrash, after his adventures in the house of Laban and after his experience with Esau, came home to the land of his fathers uninjured and 'whole' – whole in body, *shalem be-gufo*, whole in his wealth, *shalem be-mamono*, and whole in his Torah, *shalem be-torato*.

This is an illuminating comment, not only in that it provides evidence that the Rabbis, too, knew the ideal *mens sana in corpore sano*, but also in its rejection of that philosophy of the religious life which seeks to make true religion synonymous with poverty and adversity and incompatible with prosperity and success. To be sure, Judaism teaches that a person must be strong enough to meet pain and failure when they come without losing faith in God, cer- tainly, in the words of the Rabbis, not everyone merits two tables – both material and spiritual success – but our Midrash is a reminder that there is no *necessary* connection between physical disability and pain and a sound religious outlook.

Even if it be true that there is room in the wide range of Jewish religious experience for strong self-denial and asceticism, it is also true that a person can be 'whole in his Torah' without going about in rags and without presenting to the world an emaciated appear- ance, though there have been Jewish saints who have done both. The Rabbis, whose devotion to the Torah ideal has never been equalled, could yet teach that a beautiful wife, a lovely home with fine furniture, broaden a man's mind, enabling him the better to succeed in his studies.

—10—

Va-yeshev

But he refused. (Genesis 39:8)

A non-Jewish author wrote a book called *Sermons in Accents*, on the signs used in the Hebrew Bible to indicate the traditional cantillation. He rightly observed that, in addition to their musical value, the accents are a commentary to Scripture. By means of the musical notation certain words are emphasized and brought into prominence; others are brought together in a special way; joyful passages are recited with an exhilarating swing, mournful passages as a slow dirge and in this way the text is made to live in the minds of those who hear it read.

An excellent example of this interpretative role of the accents is the note on the word *va-yemaen*, the Hebrew word in our text for 'But he refused'. This is a *shalshelet* (this word means 'a chain'), a long, drawn out, wavering note, used elsewhere in the Bible for such phrases as 'and he tarried'. It seems quite incongruous here in the verse describing Joseph's refusal to sin with Potiphar's wife. Of all the notes it is the least stable. This note expresses vacillation where we would expect firm resolve.

Yet, on reflection, may it not be that this note was deliberately chosen to convey the thought that even the greatest of men does not escape from temptation without a severe internal struggle? Joseph did refuse, those responsible for the note are saying, but only after he had wrestled with his conscience; he wavered and his victory was not won lightly. According to the ancient sages, Joseph would, in fact, have yielded had he not conjured to mind the image of his father to strengthen him in his resolve.

How true to life and how realistic! What a mistake to think of the religious person, engaged in the self-discipline demanded by faith, as one who knows nothing of the anguish of giving up cherished desires; as one to whom *Sturm und Drang* are foreign. The truth of the matter is that, in Judaism at any rate, the righteous man is one who faces temptation and refuses to give in, in the full knowledge that his sacrifice will cost him dearly in terms of soul-searing agony. The greatest harm done to religious faith is caused by those who depict its adherents as beings who live in cloistered seclusion, remote from the day-to-day problems and temptations of normal existence.

Hasidim tell of a follower who was called into the presence of the Tzanzer Rov, who said to him: 'What would you do if you were to find a purse full of money?' 'Rebbe,' the man replied, 'I would, of course, return it to its rightful owner.' 'You are a fool,' said the Rebbe. Another follower was called in to the Rebbe and asked the same question. 'I am no fool,' declared this man. 'I would keep it for myself.' 'You are a scoundrel,' said the Rebbe, pushing the man out of the room. When a third follower was ushered into the Rebbe's room and the question put to him, he replied: 'Rebbe, how can I tell what I shall do when the moment of temptation comes? I may be weak and keep the purse for myself. All I can do is to pray to God that if I am ever called upon to face such a situation I may be strong enough to do the right thing.' 'You are a wise man,' said the Rebbe.

One of the reasons why the stories in the Book of Genesis are eternally fresh is because the heroes and heroines are depicted not as immaculate saints but as normal men and women with their quota of faults, some of them severe faults, but who struggle upwards towards God. The ideal religious man is he who, despite the blandishments of those forces which seek to cause him to err, can yet emerge from the struggle without yielding, so that of him it can be said, as it was said of Joseph: 'But he refused'.

—11—

Mikketz

*Then spoke the chief butler unto Pharaoh saying: 'I make
mention of my fault this day'.* (Genesis 41:9)

*But the chief butler did not remember Joseph: he forgot
him.* (Genesis 40:23)

Joseph had placed his trust in Pharaoh's chief butler, whose dream
he had interpreted for good. In return, the chief butler had promised Joseph that when he was reinstated, as foretold by Joseph, he
would mention him to Pharaoh and plead on Joseph's behalf.
However, we read, that when the chief butler had been freed from
prison, he did not remember Joseph but he forgot him. The
Hebrew idiom is expressive. When an ancient Hebrew wanted to
refer to forgetfulness he did so by using both the negative and the
positive forms. Where we say simply: 'he forgot' the ancient
Hebrew said: 'he did not remember: he forgot'. The standard commentators to the verse elaborate on this theme. Thus, Rashi
explains the repetition to mean that the chief butler did not
remember Joseph on the day he was asked to – it went in one ear
and out of the other – so, naturally, he forgot all about it when he
was reinstated. Ibn Ezra explains that the repetition means that the
chief butler did not remember Joseph by word of mouth - he did
not actually say: I will remember you' – with the result that he forgot Joseph in his heart.

All this mounts up to the important truth, simple though it is,
that if you do not remember, you forget. Psychologists have
demonstrated convincingly – and this truth seems to have been
recognized by the ancients as well – that we tend to push certain
unpleasant thoughts with disturbing implications out of our

conscious mind, with the result that, though we persuade ourselves that we are making a real effort to remember these things,
the mechanism of forgetfulness is at work all the time in the depth
of the unconscious. To take a simple example, it happens on occasion that we have a duty we are reluctant to meet to pay a visit to
a house and we forget the number of the house we intend to visit.
We all know children with bad memories with regard to their
school-work and yet the same children can reel off–apparently
without– effort lists of football or television stars.

This is without doubt why one finds so many injunctions in the
Bible to *remember*. The command to wear *tzitzit* is said to be as a
reminder of duties to God and man: 'That ye may remember and
do all My commandments and be holy to your God' (Numbers
15:49). The medieval commentator on the precepts, Aaron Halevi
of Barcelona, explained this precept by the analogy of a man who
ties a knot in his handkerchief to remind him of something he does
not wish to forget. (The fact that, when we do this, we often forget
what the knots are there for, is beside the point). In the same way
Scripture enjoins the Israelite to 'remember the Sabbath to keep it
holy' (Exodus 20:8); to remember the Exodus: 'That thou mayest
remember the day when thou camest forth out of the land of
Egypt all the days of thy life' (Deuteronomy 16:3); to remember the
history of his people: 'Remember the days of old' (Deuteronomy
32:7); and to remember God himself: 'But thou shalt remember the
Lord thy God, for it is He that giveth thee power' (Deuteronomy
8:18). The idea behind all these injunctions is that it is fatally easy
to forget duties and responsibilities unless they are prevented from
fading from the memory by an effort of the will.

Because of this Jews have a regular round of duties which they
are called upon to carry out. There are times when we tend to feel
this regularity to be oppressive. Religious emotions cannot be
turned on and off at will. There are times when Judaism demands
that we attend synagogue services, for example, when we are in no
mood for prayer. Yet without an uninterrupted sequence of duties
the means of giving expression to our deepest longings would not
be met when required, and a person would have to be spiritually
insensitive, indeed, if he never had such longings and required no
opportunity to give expression to them.

We have to admit that none of us does or can think about God
all the time. It is sheer pretence to suppose that we can or do go
about all day long thinking divine thoughts and meditating on the

great, eternal truths while engaged in our daily pursuits. However, there is, as a well-known religious thinker put it, such a thing as 'having an undercurrent of consciousness running all through a man's life and mind; such a thing as having a melody sounding in our ears perpetually, "so sweet we know not we are listening to it" until it stops and then, by the poverty of the naked and silent atmosphere, we know how musical were the sounds that we scarcely knew we heard'. Our religion is the background to our lives. The Psalmist says: 'I lift up mine eyes unto the hills' (Psalms 121:1). We are not always in the mood for ascending mountains,but they are always there to provide us with inspiration when we need it.

The Kotzker Rebbe remarked that we read in the Shema: 'And these words, which I command thee this day, shall be *upon thine heart*' – *al levavekhah* – not 'in thine heart', *bilvavekha*. For, he said, who can have thoughts of God always in his heart? The Jewish calendar, the synagogue services, the home rituals, these keep the religious memory alive, they keep the words of God *upon* our hearts,and if we use them to the full as reminders of spiritual values, as 'signposts to heaven', we firmly implant the highest ideals and the sublime thoughts *in* our hearts.

The old psychological principle of 'no impression without expression' embodied in Jewish prayer and observance has made Jewish experience emotionally vibrant and satisfying. By preserving these forms we keep our faith alive. In the words used by the commentators in describing the fault of the chief butler, by remembering on the day we do not forget later on and by remembering by word of mouth we do not forget in our hearts.

Va-yiggash

And Joseph shall put his hand upon thine eyes. (Genesis 46:4)

Jacob's sons return to him from Egypt with the good news that his beloved son Joseph is not only alive and well but is the famous ruler of all the land of Egypt, second only to the great Pharaoh. Jacob's sons wax eloquent in their telling of Joseph's great success, of the riches of his palace, of his high rank and the power he holds in his hands. Jacob silences them in words only a father can fully appreciate: 'It is enough for me that my son lives.' God appears to Jacob commanding him to be of good cheer. God promises Jacob that he will be with him in Egypt and will in the future bring his descendant back to Jacob's own land. When he goes down to Egypt, God tells him, Joseph will 'put his hand upon thine eyes'.

The standard commentators are puzzled by this expression. What does Scripture mean when it speaks of Joseph putting his hand upon his father's eyes? A plausible suggestion is that in ancient times when a man died his son put his hand on his father's eyes to close them. According to this explanation, God promises Jacob that this last service of closing the eyes would be performed by the son he has given up for dead. Yet it seems a little strange that Jacob should have been reminded of his death in the very moment of his great joy on learning that Joseph was alive and would welcome him to his palace, father and son meeting again after so many years of absence. Other commentators, therefore, understand the expression to mean that Joseph will watch over his father and his family in Egypt, taking over the cares that had devolved on Jacob, who would no longer have the need to keep his eyes open to care for the family. Joseph would take care of them all and by so doing would close Jacob's eyes by relieving him of his responsibilities.

Many years ago I heard Rabbi Babad of Vienna give the following rather far-fetched but still significant explanation. Jacob was primarily a man of vision, whereas Joseph was the supreme man of action. Even Joseph's dreams were of practical affairs, realized when he became the ruler of Egypt. Thus it can be said that Joseph's symbol was the hand while Jacob's symbol was the eye. Jacob was promised that Joseph's practical abilities, his statesman-like qualities, his 'hand', would be added to Jacob's vision of the future, his 'eyes'.

Hand and eyes, denoting the need for both a vision and the means of bringing about its realization, have to be present in the life of society. This idea is perhaps behind the Rabbinic saying that the sage is greater, in a sense, than the prophet. The tremendous vision of the Hebrew prophets of a world free from war and aggression can be brought to fruition only by sages who are aware that the ideal is remote in itself and who grapple or try to grapple with the sorry reality that is the human condition in the here and now. The Kabbalists speak of four worlds, one above the other. In one sense, the World of Action, embracing this world, is the lowest of all four Worlds. Yet in another sense the World of Action is the highest of all when it is seen as the arena in which human beings struggle to realize the good that flows from the higher Worlds.

The story of Jacob and Joseph was repeated in Jewish history throughout the ages. Jewry has always been blessed with men of vision and insight but it has also been blessed with men of action without whom the visionaries would have remained impractical idealists. Eyes and hands, Jacob and Joseph, when these combine they help to build or, at least, come nearer to building, a world in which earth is closer to heaven and heaven closer to earth.

—13—

Va-yehi

And the days of Israel drew near to die. (Genesis 47:29)

Now the days of David drew near to die. (1 Kings 2:1).

This, the literal reading of the two verses – the first in the *sidra*, the second in the Haftarah – is interpreted by the Rabbis to yield the thought that it is only the days of the righteous which pass away. The days of the righteous die; the righteous themselves live on.

Say what you will of the silence of Scripture on the subject of the afterlife. Say if you must that Judaism is a this-worldly religion. Repeat as often as you like the old gibe that religion is pie in the sky when you die, encouraging its adherents to ignore present evils in the hope of future bliss. Yet, when all has been said, it remains true that the belief in the immortality of the soul is so deeply woven into the fabric of Judaism, however the doctrine of the resurrection of the dead is understood, that any attempt to interpret the ancient faith without it is bound to result in nothing but travesty.

However, it is objected, the mind is dependent on the body. If the brain is damaged the mind is affected. How, then, can personality survive when the body has died and the brain ceases to function? Yet all the medical evidence does no more than show that the person *depends* on the brain, not that he is the product of the brain. The brain, to the religious view, is the person's instrument of the soul while it inhabits the body.

It is further objected that the belief in immortality is a greedy belief, the product of the fear in the grasping egoist not courageous enough to face with equanimity the fact of his own ultimate extinction; but immortality is not desired only, or even chiefly, for ourselves. No sane believer thinks that he alone will survive while all others will eventually die. It is when we come face to face with the death of someone we loved dearly that we find it hard to believe that one so lovely in life has been snuffed out like a candle.

Even for ourselves, surely the hope of immortality implies something more than mere endless extension of our present selves in time. Does it not rather involve the hope that somehow in the realm of eternity our highest nature, our sublimest longings, our loftiest thoughts, will find their fulfilment? Shaw and others have rightly ridiculed the notion of a heaven of harp-playing choirs endlessly repeating flat hymns of praise; but was the heaven of Judaism ever at all like this? Did not the Rabbis have a more vital conception when they described the 'Academy on High' where the saints study the Torah from the mouth of God? Is not the Rabbinic saying, that scholars have rest neither in this world nor the next, a subtle anticipation of Shaw's *bon mot* that the best definition of Hell is a perpetual holiday?

Given the belief in God, the belief in the soul's immortality is unavoidable. Can we seriously believe that all the mighty strivings of human beings; their slow climb to civilization, still not realized on earth; their reaching out haltingly to God and God reaching down in response; their goodness; their search for truth are all doomed to ultimate oblivion? Can we believe that the benevolent Creator has created only eventually to destroy? Or is it not a more reasonable faith which holds that nothing worthwhile is permanently lost, that no good deed is forgotten and no worthy thought passes into the void?

Certainly Judaism encourages us to live in 'one world at a time'. Of course one of the aims of our religion is the establishment of the Kingdom of Heaven here on earth. Yet behind and beyond and embracing the Jewish ideal of this-worldly service is the assurance of immortality to give humans the conviction that they 'labour not in vain' and that what they do with their lives is of eternal significance.

PART THREE
EXODUS/*SHEMOT*

Shemot

The Book of Exodus is called, in Hebrew, *Shemot*, after the opening verse: 'Now these are the names of the children of Israel', followed by a list of the names of Jacob's sons, the ancestors of the twelve tribes of Israel.

Lists of names occur frequently in the Bible and there is an abundance of evidence that high significance is attached to individual names. To this day, every child is given a Jewish name; a boy at the *brit*, a girl when her father is called up in the synagogue. It appears, however, that in the early Rabbinic period some Jews had Greek or Roman names. Even one of the early Rabbinic figures was called Antigonus and a pupil of Rabbi Meir was called Symachus. No doubt the Midrashic, anachronistic comment on 'these are the names of the children of Israel' castigates Jews who gave their children non-Jewish names. The Midrash (Leviticus Rabba 32: 5) states that when the Israelites came out of Egypt they still retained the names of their ancestors who went down there. 'They did not call Judah "Leon", nor Reuben "Rufus", nor Benjamin "Alexander".'

Why are names so significant? A name is a means of identification, a manner of asserting the uniqueness of each individual. Reuben is Reuben and Simeon is Simeon. It is no accident that prisoners are depersonalized by their being given numbers rather than names, though it is certainly not in the spirit of Judaism to degrade people by depriving them of their specific characteristics. When the Talmud notes that angels in the Bible have no names (except for the names Michael and Gabriel in the later books) it is precisely because angels are seen as performing certain functions without possessing any real personalities of their own.

Animals, too, have no names. One dog does not differ from another dog in the way that Reuben differs from Simeon and

Simeon from Reuben. (The practice, nowadays, of giving names to pets is, of course, anthropomorphic, endowing animals with human significance, though it is harmless in itself.)

It belongs to the dignity and supreme worth of human beings that no two are alike. As the ancient Rabbis remark, just as no two human beings have exactly the same facial appearance (identical twins are only an apparent exception) so are the qualities of their hearts and minds different.

It is a gross canard which states that Judaism knows only of group identity. The lie is given to this notion by the very emphasis in the Bible on the listing of names. It can all be seen as a mighty protest against totalitarian attempts to efface individuality.

There is an old regulation that a synagogue should have twelve windows corresponding to the twelve tribes, each with its own window to Heaven. One might add that each member of each particular tribe has its own fragment of the divine light which only he or she can reveal. Reuben cannot achieve that for which Simeon was created, neither can Simeon do that for which Reuben was created.

A Midrashic comment has it that the 'hard labour' to which the Egyptians subjected the Israelites, involved, among other onerous tasks, making weak men carry loads suitable only for strong men, and strong men carry loads suitable for weak men.

To compel a weak man to carry a load too heavy for him is undoubtedly an act of torture; but why should it be considered hard labour to compel a man to carry a load less than he can bear?

For the Rabbis of the Midrash, what is really at stake is human dignity. It degrades a strong man and affects his emotional stab-ility when, by giving him too easy a task to perform, it is implied that he is incapable of anything better. Even among slaves building the pyramids there might have been something akin to what we call today job satisfaction if the demands had presented a challenge. Then, at least, they would have consoled themselves with the fact that they were doing something hard but perhaps worthwhile. There was, however, only frustration and bitterness when they were obliged to perform tasks that gave them no opportunity to realize their human potential.

A similar point was made, about animals, by a medieval French commentator, who said that the prohibition against ploughing with an ox and an ass yoked together is not – as some say – because it is cruel to the ass, but rather because it is cruel to the ox, which, capable of far greater effort and power, has to be yoked with a beast capable of much less.

In the history of Jewish learning, it is not only students who take on subjects too advanced for them who become bored with their studies and eventually give them up entirely. Students who tackle easy, unchallenging subjects when capable of mastering more profound ones also become bored.

This applies to Jewish life as a whole. Teachers of Judaism do well to present it in as attractive a manner as possible, but they should never forget that the real attraction of a living religion is presented by the demands it makes, and the challenge it presents, to those who are sufficiently large of spirit and stout of heart to shoulder the heavier burden.

—15—

Va-era

And Moses spoke so unto the children of Israel; but they hearkened not unto Moses for impatience of spirit, and for cruel bondage. (Exodus 6:9)

The lack of response on the part of his oppressed people to Moses' message of hope and redemption is one of the most poignant incidents in the history of the Jewish people. The great leader comes to the downtrodden Hebrews with the joyful tidings that their God has heard their cry for help, but to his dismay they turn a deaf ear to the stirring news. They do not even bother to listen.

Disappointing and tragic though it is, Scripture is quick to point out the reason for the failure of Moses' message to penetrate to the hearts of the people. They were a slave people; many bitter years of bondage and oppression had paralysed their will, they had learnt, as slaves do, to think only in terms of immediate survival; the vision of a life of freedom was beyond their spiritual and emotional grasp.

The ancient story is re-enacted today in the comparative failure of the message of Judaism to make itself heard and elicit a response. Judaism always had to struggle for its existence; its adherents have had to be in the forefront of the battle ever since it first brought to mankind the new message of human duties to the God of justice and righteousness, of mercy and and compassion. But in spite of its many vicissitudes, it is doubtful whether Judaism has ever had to face the indifference to its teachings it faces after the Emancipation. What is the reason for modern man's indifference to religion? Our text gives the answer: 'But they hearkened not unto Moses, for impatience of spirit and for cruel bondage.'

The Hebrew original for 'impatience of spirit' is *kotzer ruah* and can bear the translation 'shortness of spirit' or 'lack of spirit'.

Judaism, like other religions, experienced a crisis in the twentieth century. The nineteenth-century problem of science versus religion had been engaged in and it became obvious that there was no real conflict. It was certainly no question of victory on either side but it became perfectly respectable for scientists to be religious and believers to be scientists. Then there were two world wars, the Holocaust, mass murder in so many places with terrible weapons unimaginable in former ages. Yet the reactions of men and women of spirit to these horrors have awakened a mighty protest against moral relativism; the spirit of man refuses to bow to the gods of chaos.

The second reason for the rejection of the message of Judaism is given in the second part of our text. The Hebrew words *avodah kashah*, translated as 'cruel bondage', mean literally 'hard labour' and, in terms of Jews living in today's world, they express the many distractions of modern life, the difficult struggle for existence even in a world of plenty, and, for Jews, the severe economic problems often associated with religious observances.

Yet here too there is room for hope. Despite the pessimists a better, more just world has been slowly emerging. Already the bad old days of child labour in the mines, of harsh treatment of the poor and the alien belong, as a philosophy of life, to the past.

Like our ancestors, we must learn to rise, despite previous failures, above the hindrances of *kotzer ruah* and *avodah kashah* to embrace the full spiritual life of the Jewish religion, without hankering after any spurious spirituality that involves in itself *kotzer ruah*.

16

Bo

*This month shall be unto you the beginning of months: it
shall be the first month of the year to you.* (Exodus 12:2)

The month in which the Exodus took place – later called the month
of Nisan – was to become the first month of the calendar. This significance attached to the first month (during which there took
place the renewal of the Hebrew people, from slaves to free
men)contains the message of the need for renewal and rejuvenation in Jewish life. The very word for month, *hodesh*, means 'that
which is new', referring to the new moon. Each month a Jew is
expected to attempt to review and amend his life and to make his
contribution of bringing into Jewish life fresh vigour and a new
approach. Constant renewal is the secret of Jewish survival.

The striving for that which is new is fundamental to human
nature. Human beings are constantly searching for new experiences, for novel ideas and for the variety that is the spice of life.

In the realm of the intellect the original thinker is assured of a
sympathetic hearing. Even in religious matters each generation
requires and demands a fresh approach to eternal truth. Old arguments and modes of religious thought, effective enough in medieval
times, are often unconvincing today, since thought has moved on.
With a profound appreciation of this the ancient Rabbis pointed out
that Scripture says: 'If ye shall hearken diligently unto My commandments which I command you this day...' (Deuteronomy
11: 3). This is to teach, say the Rabbis, that each day the Torah should
be seen as if it had been given afresh, that is, the Torah has a new
message for each 'day', each epoch in human history, or so at least
can the saying of the Rabbis be homiletically interpreted.

It was this thought that filled keen students of the Torah with the urge to discover new ideas enshrined with the old. Every diligent student of the Torah would exercise his creative talents in his attempt to discover new truths, *hiddushey torah* which, as the Rabbis teach, were new and yet implicit in the age-old Torah.

It is therefore quite wrong to speak of Judaism as a hide bound system, fossilized, living in the past and incapable of growth. To be sure, Judaism teaches that there are imperishable values and eternal truths, binding for all time; but in each age there is the need for each age to make these truths available to that particular age and such a task involves both renewal and reinterpretation.

Modern Judaism has suffered from two extremes in its approach to modernism and post-Modernism. On the one hand there are the extreme conservatives, who have drawn a halo of sanctity around every detail of the life of our ancestors, who look with dismay at the slightest departure from that way of life. These ancestor-worshippers have no use for anything new. For them, all the good things were found in the good old days alone and contemporaries should only seek to emulate the great heroes and heroines who lived then. This attitude has an undoubted appeal to many Jews but it has done incalculable damage to Judaism by identifying an eternal faith with a passing phase of existence. It has allowed the idea to gain ground among young Jews that Judaism is foreign and of little relevance to the modern world; and post-modernism, while impatient with some aspects of modernism, is equally impatient, or should be, with some aspects of medievalism. There is no going back. At the other extreme are those with no reverence for the sacred traditions of Judaism, who would destroy much of the old way of life in order to be up-to-date at all costs.

The Jewish ideal is to preserve all that is true and of value in the old without sacrificing the natural human striving for originality and creativity. Many years ago a process was discovered by means of which the Old Masters in the National Gallery could be cleaned. At first there were strong protests against the 'sacrilege'. Many of the protesters seemed to have considered the very grime that had accumulated through the ages to be an essential part of the pictures. Others argued that the Masters did their work so as to be finally revealed in the way in which they appear after centuries. The protests went unheeded, the pictures were cleaned, the grime removed, and new beauties, previously obscured, were revealed to the eye.

We ought to keep this in mind in our approach to the question of renewal. We should never identify the dust of ages with the living Jewish faith, but when attempting to remove the dust we need to be ever vigilant not to wreak irreparable damage on the picture of Judaism by a too vigorous and misapplied process of cleansing. As has so often been said, Jews today need serenity of mind to accept that which cannot be changed, courage to change that which can and should be changed, and, above all, the wisdom to distinguish one from the other.

There is an interesting regulation concerning the obligation to eat unleavened bread at Passover. The Rabbis rule on the basis of those Scriptural verses in which the duty of eating *matzah* is ordained, are juxtaposed with verses stating that *hametz* is forbidden, that *matzah* is valid for the *mitzvah* only if made from dough that can become *hametz*. Dough of wheat, barley or oats, which can ferment to become *matzah*, may be used as such; but dough of rice or millet, which cannot ferment properly and hence can never become *hametz*, cannot be used for the *mitzvah*.

There is far more to this regulation than a rule based on a juggling of texts. In many Rabbinic passages rules are expressed with important religious and moral truths quite apart from the rules themselves. With regard to our rule, what the Rabbis were saying is that life is good, that this world in which we live can be a very beautiful and wonderful place, that human nature is not basically evil but can be good, and that opportunities are given to man to develop every aspect of his being.

The ancient sages were sufficiently realistic to recognize that man has an evil as well as a good side to his nature. They spoke of the evil side, the *yetzer ha-ra*, as 'the yeast in the dough', as that which causes fermentation of the heart, so to speak, but, in characteristic Jewish fashion, that even this is not without value. Consequently, it can in no way be said that to be a fulfilment of God's purpose a man should shut himself away from society in something like a hermitage or monastery. The good life, as conceived by the majority of Jewish teachers, is lived in society. Of course, the man who lives a life in the company of others may fall by the wayside, may succumb to temptation to a far greater extent than the man who lives in solitude, or who boasts that his 'faith is not of this world'. However, without the possibility of evil there can be no lasting good; or, in the symbolic language of the Rabbis, *matzah* can be made only from dough that can become *hametz*.

The point has often been made that Judaism refuses to divide life too neatly into the secular and the sacred. All life can be hallowed if it is infused with soul. 'The Torah was not given to the ministering angels' is the realistic assessment of human nature by the Rabbis. Life must not be exploited; nor must it be denied. It should rather be consecrated; or, at least, this is the message of normative Judaism, that the Kingdom of Heaven be realized on earth.

The impressive words at the end of the first creation narrative in the Book of Genesis – 'And God saw everything that He had made, and, behold, it was very good' – are thus interpreted in the Rabbinic Midrash. The Midrash states that 'good' in the verse refers to man's good inclination ,whereas 'very good' refers to the evil inclination. For without the evil inclination the world could not endure; or, to put it in the language of our day, without life's ebb and flow, without the tensions resulting from the constant struggle against evil, without ambition and the need for self-fulfilment, life would be a very colourless affair. It might be *good* but it could hardly be *very* good.

One day mankind will surely learn that true religion is not synonymous with the hatred of life. One day we will all come to appreciate that it is the divine will that we enjoy in the marvellous world He has created. One day it will be realized that *matzah* can be made only from dough that can become *hametz*. With such a realization, Judaism, as a faith in which God is worshipped and thanked for His bounty, will come into its own.

17

Beshallah

A famous nineteenth-century Jewish preacher noted that in the description of the crossing of the Red Sea the Bible, in one verse, speaks of the Israelites walking 'through the sea on dry ground', in another verse of their walking 'on dry ground through the sea'. His interpretation was as follows.

The Midrash points out that the sea was not divided as soon as the Israelites entered it. At first it seemed that the few brave men who leapt into the sea at the command of God would be drowned. Though the waters did not part, these men waded deeper and deeper into the waves undaunted by the threat to their lives. It was not until the words of the Psalmist: 'Save me O God; for the waters have come into my soul' were uttered by them that the waters were divided and the people were able to walk through on the dry ground. Of the heroes who leapt into the sea, the verse states that they walked 'through the sea on the dry ground' – at first they walked in the sea and only after they had demonstrated their trust in God did they walk on dry ground. Not so the more timid of their brethren, the men of little faith. They waited on the shore, refusing to venture forth until the waters were divided: they walked on dry ground in the midst of the sea.

So it has been throughout the ages. Progress has been possible only because of the heroic efforts of ardent pioneers who dared everything in obedience to the voice of God. At first they were ridiculed, condemned and persecuted, while those who benefited from their self-sacrifice and devotion looked on without making the slightest effort to help. Only after victory had been won, did these others begin to tread with ease the path smoothed for them in anguish and with tears.

How many examples of this we have in Jewish history! Amos braving the wrath of a powerful king and influential high priest; Rabbi Akiba suffering a martyr's death for the sake of the Torah; Maimonides, risking unpopularity and the charge of heresy for the sake of his deep insights into Judaism; the Hasidim accepting with equanimity the bitter calumnies heaped upon them in their zeal for the new path leading to a rejuvenation of religious life; Herzl allowing himself to be branded an impossible visionary for the sake of his people – all of these were men who brought blessing, hope, courage and dignity into the lives of countless Jews who, such is the irony of fate, learned to appreciate their efforts only after the sacrifice had been made and the victory assured.

Of course, not everyone who treads a new path is right and deserves credit. There have been men fired with pioneering zeal whom it would have been folly to have followed. We owe it to ourselves and to mankind to investigate carefully the claims of the innovator and to be satisfied before we follow him that the path he treads leads in the direction we desire and ought to go.

Until we gain this conviction we are justified, indeed we are duty bound, to hold our enthusiasm in check; but when, like our people of old, we hear the call to move onwards and we hold back out of cowardice or indifference, when we fear to get our feet wet when the pioneers are ready to drown for the faith we and they hold dear, it is then that our attitude is ignoble.

ACKNOWLEDGING THE MIRACLE

The great Musar teacher, Rabbi E. E. Dessler, was fond of pointing to the Midrashic statement that when the waters of the Red Sea were parted, waters all over Egypt were parted. Even the water in Egyptian kitchen bowls was miraculously divided. Similarly, the Midrash states, when the very old and barren matriarch, Sarah, miraculously gave birth to a child, all barren, old women gave birth to children. Men and women of faith at the time would say: 'Because of the miracle of the parting of the sea and because of the miracle of Sarah giving birth, all waters were parted as an offshoot of the former miracle and all barren women were blessed with children as an offshoot of the latter miracle.' The sceptic, on the other hand, will argue that these miracles are not really miracles at all. Look and see, the sceptic in the time of the Red Sea would say;

undoubtedly something odd is going on, but it must be a natural happening since the water in the bowl in the kitchen has also been divided.

The whole question of miracles is now seen to depend on how we look at life. For God to intervene directly in human life – which is what is implied in the notion of miracle – He must do so with a degree of room for doubt, otherwise the manifestation of His power would so convince the sceptic that disbelief would be impossible and faith a mere mechanical response. There must always be the possibility to explain away the miracle. Faith, like beauty, is in the eye of the beholder; or, as the Hafetz Hayyim once said: For those who have faith there are no problems. For those who have no faith there are no solutions.

18

Yitro

In the third month after the children of Israel were gone
forth out of the land of Egypt, the same day came they into
the wilderness of Sinai. (Exodus 19:1)

There is an interesting comment on this verse by the Rabbis. They
noted that Scripture says *bayom hazeh*, 'on this day', they came to
Sinai, not, as we might have expected, *bayom hahu*, 'on that day'.
This is to teach, say the Rabbis, that the words of the Torah must
always be as vital and as fresh to us as on the day of the original
revelation.

That is to say, the Jew should not speak of his ancestors arriving
at Sinai on that day – in the remote past – but on this day, the
unforgiving present. The Torah is in harmony with the idea of
progress and is always relevant to the special needs of each age.

This Rabbinic comment gives us the key to understanding the
basic difference between the Jewish approach to the tremendous
event of the revelation and that of other faiths and other schools of
thought. Few thinking people desire to deny the value of the
Hebraic element in Western civilization or to minimize the importance of the legacy of Israel.

Yet to the adherents of other faiths, these contributions are
things of the past; Israel, they hold, did, indeed, come to Sinai in
those days – *bayom hahu*. However, for the Jew the Torah has never
been superseded; it is not ancient history, not a museum piece or a
fossil, but a living religion, with the capacity to renew itself constantly. Israel receives the Torah afresh each day – *bayom hazeh*.

Christianity and Islam have long taught that a new
dispensation has taken the place of the old Torah of Israel. Under
the influence of these religions few serious students of religion saw

any need to reckon with, much less to understand, Judaism. Only in comparatively recent years have non-Jewish scholars begun to give earnest thought to the content and application of Judaism and to the appreciation of the riches contained in our ancient literatures, and even these worthy scholars study Judaism as they would study any other branch of ancient literature, as they would examine the antiquities of Greece and Rome, of Egypt, Assyria and Babylonia. They do not admit (why should they, granted that for them Judaism is not a live option?) that the ancient wisdom of the Torah is a relevant force in the religious life of mankind, or that Judaism possesses continuity. They forget that Judaism is still the living faith of a living people.

Unfortunately, a similar attitude of mind to that of our detractors is shown by some of our own people. Many worthy Jews appear to look upon the Torah as something which could adequately have been followed only in days of old. This attitude is seen both by those who claim that the Torah was possible of fulfilment only when Jews lived in a closed community in the Ghetto and by those who argue that the Torah, while giving preservative value for Jewish life in the Diaspora, has little to say in the new life of Israel restored to its ancient homeland, as if Judaism were not an eternal faith but an old-fashioned way of life, ideally suited for the unsophisticated old folks who knew no better.

In our festivals we recite the benediction 'Who has kept us alive, and preserved us, and enabled us to reach this season'. We are glad to live in this season, *bizeman hazeh*. We do not ask God to keep us always in the good old days. It is new life that we desire and our Torah has its specific message for that new life.

Also, let it be noted, the full implications of the revelation at Sinai were not completely realized or even fully understood until much later in human history. In a sense the Torah was incapable of fulfilment in the culture in which it was given. In that distant age the state of human society was such that only a gradual unfolding of God's purpose as history developed could have brought about the realization of that purpose.

Maimonides gives expression to this truth when he writes of God gradually leading the Israelites away from primitive notions of religion. In their state of civilization, Maimonides writes, it was not possible to show them the whole truth right away. God did not lead the Israelites 'the way of the land of the Philistine for it was near'.

In the realm of the spirit, progress is made surely but slowly.

This can be seen from the attitude of Judaism towards polygamy and slavery. In the ancient world these two institutions were unchallenged by even the most enlightened thinkers. It has even been argued that without the institution of slavery ancient society could not have endured. For the Torah to have attempted suddenly to precipitate the Israelites into forms of social life thousands of years in advance of their time would have been to deal too violently with human nature. God preferred to work in a gradual manner. Instead of the Torah forbidding these two institutions, the Torah so regulated them and so exercised control over them that in later society they were purged of many of their most offensive characteristics, until, eventually and under the influence of the Hebraic ideal, they were completely abolished, in the Western world at least.

It would be true to say that the purpose of the Torah with regard to slavery was not fully realized until the abolition of slavery in the eighteenth and nineteenth centuries. Indeed, as long as there exist forced labour and labour camps, the Torah's purpose is still unfulfilled. We can also truly say that when, after centuries of Jewish teaching upholding the ideal of monogamy, Rabbenu Gershom banned polygamy in the year 1000, in that year our people came once again to Sinai. And so throughout Jewish and general history, the closer human institutions approximated to the ideals of the Torah the nearer human beings came to Sinai.

19

Mishpatim

This part of the Torah follows the part describing the theophany at Sinai and the giving of the Ten Commandments. The Ten Commandments are in the nature of broad general principles. Yet for these principles to be applied in real life, detailed regulations are required and it is these that are given in this *sidra*, the first of the three great law codes in the Torah (the other two are in Leviticus and Deuteronomy).

As Judaism developed in the Talmudic period, Jewish teachings were divided into two distinct categories. The first, of which the various laws in our part as well as the Rabbinic elaboration of these, came to be known as the Halakhah, representing the whole legal side of the Jewish religion. The second category came to be known as the Aggadah, a comprehensive term embracing all the non-legal teachings and the Rabbinic elaborations on these. In Bialik's delineation, Halakhah is the prose of Judaism, Aggadah its poetry. This *sidra* provides, then, an opportunity for a brief discussion of the role and importance of the Halakhah.

The Halakhah has been subjected over the years to a barrage of criticism, much of it ill-informed, from the attacks to be found in the Gospels to the strictures of later Christian theologians. It is also true that Jews themselves have sometimes been impatient with the Halakhah and have preferred to interpret Judaism chiefly in terms of the Aggadah. The claim is made at times that while the Aggadah is broad and free, the Halakhah is inflexible and stifling, crushing the religious spirit by imposing on Jews a host of detailed laws and regulations.

Now it must be admitted that a religious approach which lays so much stress on practice is prone to peculiar temptations by its very nature. It is also true that there are devout Jews who faithfully observe all the minutiae of Jewish law without being too much aware of its spirit, but it is grossly unfair to judge the Halakhah by occasional misinterpretations and aberrations, rather than by the attitues of the great advocates and deeply spiritual teachers. If we do the latter we can see how false is the picture of Halakhic Judaism as a soul-crippling burden. On the contrary, it is the Halakhah that gives concrete expression to the yearnings of the soul by creating and applying laws that are the vehicles for spirituality.

A modern poet, speaking of the antithesis between the lawyer and the poet, wrote:

> The law the lawyers know about
> Is property and land;
> But why the leaves are on the trees,
> And why the waves disturb the seas,
> Why honey is the food of bees,
> Why horses have such tender knees,
> Why winters come when rivers freeze,
> Why Faith is more than what one sees,
> And Hope survives the worst disease,
> And Charity is more than these,
> They do not understand.

How far all this is true is a matter for debate, but one thing is certain. In Jewish thought the demarcation line between poetry and law, between the letter of the law and its spirit, between Halakhah and Aggadah, is never too finely drawn. The great source of the Halakhah, the Talmud, does in fact contain, in addition to law proper, theories and discussions on why leaves are on the trees and why honey is the food of bees, as well as profound inquiries into the nature of faith, hope and charity. Similarly, all the famed Halakhists have urged the need for inwardness in the religious life. Among the laws in our portion of the Torah are the need to show compassion to the widow and the orphan; to pay a workman on time; to care for dumb animals; to practise justice and pursue mercy; all as ways of realizing the ideals set forth by the Hebrew prophets. This is the legacy of the much-maligned Pharises, the original teachers of the Halakhah who taught how to give concrete expression to the visions of the prophets. As Pofessor Finkelstein has put it: 'Pharisaism is Prophetism in action.'

The list of laws in this portion of the Torah is prefaced by the words: 'These are the rules that you shall set before them' (Exodus 21:1). Some commentators understand 'set before them' to mean that Moses should explain the laws.

In the history of Jewish codification of laws, the laws are set out in an order and sequence that make the laws more readily intelligible. The very nature of the most authoritative of the codes is called 'The Arranged Table'; that is to say: all the laws scattered throughout the Talmud and other early sources are set out like food on a table to be eaten on the spot.

The Biblical commentator, A. B. Ehrlich, throws a different light on the expression 'set before them'. According to Ehrlich, the meaning is that Moses was first to ask the people if they approved of the laws; as if to say, God does not impose on people arbitrary laws which they accept solely in blind obedience. God rather knows what is best, but it is still essential for the people to accept freely what He demands.

That is why the medieval Jewish philosophers attempted to provide reasons for the precepts of the Torah. These thinkers were really affirming that God is no tyrannical ruler compelling unwilling subjects to obey meaningless obligations. Obedience to God's will is, of course, paramount, but, in the name of obedience itself, it cannot be imposed solely from without.

The Rabbis do speak of the yoke of the commandments but it is a yoke willingly borne by Jews of loving and caring heart and mind. This is the Jewish answer to the Pauline critique of Jewish legalism. In the language of the evening prayer: 'They praised and gave thanksgiving unto His name, and willingly accepted His sovereignty.'

In some circles, the Halakhah is presented with a 'theirs not to reason why' atttitude. Such an attitude does poor service to a system that has survived and works well precisely because of its dynamism and flexibility. What Heschel dubbed 'pan-Halakhism' can itself only be defended on extra-Halakhic grounds. To the question: 'Why keep the Halakhah?', one cannot reply: 'Because the Halakhah says so.' In other words, beneath the mind of every distinguished Halakhist and of every Jew loyal to the Halakhah, the poetic soul of an Aggadist demands that its voice, too, must be heard.

20

Terumah

*And let them make Me a sanctuary, that I may dwell
among them.* (Exodus 25:8)

This verse, on the face of it, contradicts the verse in the book of
Isaiah (66:1) in which the prophet says: 'Thus saith the Lord: The
heaven is My throne, And the earth is My footstool; Where is the
house that ye may build unto Me? And where is the place that may
be My resting-place?' The apparent contradiction between the two
verses strikes one immediately. The prophet states that God is so
far above earth and even heaven that no house can be built for
Him. And yet, in our verse from Exodus, the command is given
that the children of Israel should build a sanctuary for God to
dwell in their midst.

The Midrash deals with this question. According to the Midrash,
Moses asked in astonishment: 'Behold, heaven and the heaven and
the heaven of heaven cannot contain Thee, how, then, can we build
a house for Thy glory?' God replies: 'I do not ask what is due to Me,
but only that which is in the power of the
people to do. Twenty boards in the north, twenty to the south, eight
to the west, and I will concentrate My Shekhinah in their midst.'

In other words, God must not be thought of as entirely outside
or beyond the universe. Whenever human beings try to live the
good life, when they try to reach out to God, it is God working
through them and empowering them to conduct themselves right-
eously. Religion, to adopt Whitehead's terms, is not only a coercive
principle; it is a persuasive principle. God does not only speak and
command from without, as it were. He speaks in the recesses of the
soul. The mystical idea of the divine spark in man conveys something of this correlation between God and humans.

It is exceedingly difficult to speak of God. Human language cannot give expression to the Unfathomable. For all that, humans have always found themselves compelled haltingly to say something about God, at least in their worship of Him. In Jewish literature, two metaphors are used of God. In the favourite Yom Kippur hymn God is described as a potter shaping his clay to the patterns and forms he desires. However, there is a different metaphor favoured by the Rabbis in which God is spoken of as the Soul of the universe and He is compared with the human soul in the body: 'Just as the Holy One fills the world so the soul fills the body. Just as the Holy One sees and is not seen so the soul sees but is not itself seen. Just as the Holy One sustains the whole world so the soul sustains the body. Just as the Holy One is pure so the soul is pure. Just as the Holy One dwells in the innermost recesses so the soul dwells in the innermost recesses. Let that which possesses these five qualities come and praise Him who possesses these five qualities.' The Kabbalists teach that God surrounds all the world and yet fills all worlds.

All this is relevant to the synagogue. The synagogue is sometimes spoken of as the house of God, though in one Talmudic passage disapproval is voiced against this nomenclature; but it is still worthwhile to consider what meaning can be given to the idea that God is to be found *in* the synagogue. This cannot mean that God actually resides in the synagogue – what could 'reside' mean in such a context? The meaning is rather that the synagogue, if it carries out its task successfully, in bringing worshippers therein nearer to the divine, becomes the house in which God is found in human aspiration. As the Rabbis say, Scripture does not say that God will dwell in the midst of the sanctuary but 'in their midst', that is, in the midst of the people.The fuller meaning of a synagogue is that when men and women set aside a special, dedicated place in which they worship together as a company; where they link their lives to the past and future of their people; where they can be inspired by the beauty of the prayers and be stirred by the melodies both sad and joyous; where they can learn something of Jewish teaching, they become more aware of the spiritual side of life.

> *And thou shalt make the boards for the tabernacle of acacia*
> *wood, standing up.* (Exodus 26:15)

The boards are the pillars which held up the curtained roof of the Tabernacle. They were to be *omedim*, translated as 'standing up'.

The commentators differ as to the meaning of this expression. Some see it as a reference to the living tree, that is to say, the boards must not be taken from a fallen tree but from a living tree, cut down while it is still growing, while it *stands*, and the boards then made from that tree.

Others take it to mean that the boards must be placed in a vertical rather than a horizontal position. This would, however, be too obvious to require stating, since the whole purpose of the boards is to hold up the curtained covering, unless it means that the boards have to be perfectly straight, not sloping towards the centre.

The Rabbinic interpretation of 'standing up' is that the cut and planed boards are to be placed in the Tabernacle in the direction in which they grew on the tree, not upside down. From this the Rabbis derive the general principle that the precepts have to be carried out with objects as they grow naturally. For instance, a *lulav* and *etrog* on Sukkot must not be held upside down.

A further Rabbinic rule is that when the Tabernacle was set up again after it had been dismantled for the journeys, each board had to be put in exactly the same place it had occupied at the previous setting up of the Tabernacle. It was wrong to have, say, a northern set up on a subsequent encampment in the south, or a southern board in the north.

The notion that even inanimate boards have their rights and therefore their rightful place, that they are entitled to demand to be set up in the manner of their growth and in the special position they have won for themselves, is, on the face of it, no more than poetic fancy. Blocks of wood have neither rights nor feelings.

What is behind it all, however, is that fairness, even with regard to objects where the concept is meaningless, is a way of reminding humans of truth they otherwise would be in danger of overlooking.

The positioning of the boards denotes that, in the worship of God, human nature is not thwarted but assisted in growth and that no human being is forced by religion out of his proper place to occupy a place foreign to him.

21

Tetzaveh

And thou shalt make holy garments for Aaron thy brother,
for splendour and for beauty.   (Exodus 28:2)

The Rabbis, interpreting the prescriptions governing the dress of
the priests, ruled that the priest had to have his garments made to
measure. They were not to be too long nor too short, nor was a
priest allowed to wear a garment that was too long even if he
adjusted it at the waist. The fit of the priest's robes had to be a perfect one.

This is possibly no more than an elementary rule of aesthetics.
It was obviously objectionable for a custodian of the Temple to go
about his tasks in ill-fitting garments. However, in view of the
importance of symbolism in the Temple rituals, is it too fanciful to
follow those who interpret this rule as a reminder that the spiritual garb we wear in God's service ought to be in accordance with
the development of our character and personality; that in our religious life we ought not to aim too high nor too low? Aiming too
low is a common human failing. People cannot find spiritual sus-
tenance in an impoverished faith which makes no demands on its
adherents and has no power to inspire. When the Jews of Eastern
Europe said: 'It is hard to be a Jew', they were doing more than
expressing whimsically the difficulties of Jewish observance. They
knew that it belonged to the glory of Judaism that the religion
required the surrender of the self in the service of the highest. The
spirit of true religion is forged on the anvil of self-transcendence.
'A man's reach should exceed his grasp or what's a heaven for?' A
less common but equally stultifying fault in religion is to aim too
high. How many people torture themselves by setting themselves
ideals they are incapable of realizing! Our ideals should be hard

enough to provide a challenge but not so hard a s to make us to give up the struggle in despair. A Hasidic teacher said: 'If too much force is exercised when turning on the tap the water will gush into the glass and simply pour out again. Only through a gradual flow can the glass be filled.'

> Our religion, to be really significant, should be seen as a glorious dream of life as it can be, spurring us on in ever greater efforts. But it should also be seen as a dream capable of realization, not a beckoning mirage we can never reach. Only when our spiritual garments are suited to our measure can we minister worthily in the Temple of the Lord.

Ki Tissa

The rich shall not give more.(Exodus 30: 15)

The Talmud records an interesting controversy between the two sects of the Pharisees and the Sadducees in Temple times. The aristocratic Sadducees argued that, despite the tradition that each Jew had to give his donation of half a shekel, from which sum the perpetual offering was bought, a wealthy individual could, if he so desired, offer to defray the total cost of the offering out of his own pocket. The more democratic Pharisees refused to allow this. Every Jew, they taught, must have his share in the daily sacrifice, the wealthy not paying more, nor the poor less. The view of the Pharisees was finally adopted, and an important blow was struck for the small man in danger of being ousted by powerful competitors even from direct participation in the sacrificial system.

Few things can be more typical of the justice and fairness of the Jewish spirit than the outcome of this ancient debate. For the Jew has always been ready to apply the importance of little things and small beginnings:

> *The Lord did not set His love upon you, nor choose you,*
> *because ye were more in number than any other people —*
> *for ye were the fewest of all peoples.* (Deuteronomy 7:7)

The world has not as yet appreciated this idea to the full. Even respected thinkers are guilty of the philistinism which can find value only in mere quantity. A shocking example of this kind of vulgarity and lack of perception was H. G. Wells's 'reminder' many years ago that in order to keep our sense of proportion we must realize that Solomon's temple was a very small place which could easily have fitted within the confines of a small village church. As if the physical size mattered in assessing an institution the values of which are spiritual.

Another example of modern intellectual caprice in matters of size is the frequent suggestion that because of the vastness of the universe revealed by the new cosmology, the older religious conceptions of man's place in the scheme of things and his ultimate destiny have been effectively exploded. In ancient and medieval times, it is suggested, when the earth was held to be fixed, with the sun and the planets revolving round it, it was easy to believe in the uniqueness of man; but now that science has convincingly shown man's home to be an insignificant speck in the vastnesses of space, how can man delude himself into thinking that his life and his achievements are of importance?

Yet a few moments of real thinking on this question will immediately demonstrate the vulgarity and superficiality of the argument. True our earth is microscopically small, but, so far as we know, human life has nowhere else appeared. Puny man on his tiny planet can weigh and measure and describe the tremendous universe but the universe can do none of these things. True that we now have a deeper understanding of the Psalmist's word: 'What is man that Thou art mindful of him?' (Psalms 8:4) but we must not forget that the Psalmist goes on to say: 'Yet Thou hast made him a little lower than the angels, and hast crowned him with glory and honour' (verse 5). Far from the immense size of the universe destroying man's faith, it can be an aid to that faith, its contemplation filling him with the sense of wonder, of awe, of humility, and of understanding, all of which provide most fertile soil for the growth of religious feeling.

The lesson of the importance of small things will not be lost on Jews who, throughout their history, have constantly been obliged to start again from small beginnings. From their rich experience throughout the ages, Jews have come to appreciate the truth of the words: 'Though thy beginning was small, yet thy end should greatly increase (Job 8:7).

Moses knew not that the skin of his face sent forth beams.
(Exodus 34:29)

Moses' shining face – 'beams of glory' is the expression used by the Rabbis – has been a constant theme in both literature and art. The Midrash has its own way of portraying the significance of this strange phenomenon. The tablets of stone which Moses brought down from Sinai, states the Midrash, were six hand-breadths in size. Two hand-breadths were held by Moses, two by God and there were two in the middle. It was from the two in the middle that Moses obtained his beams of glory. This fanciful Midrash gives expression to a profound truth.

Two hand-breadths of the tablets are in the hands of God; that is to say, there is an element of mystery about religious faith which imparts grandeur to it. God is incomprehensible; the Source and Creator of all being is hidden from human gaze. Man's finite mind cannot hope to grasp the Infinite. An essential ingredient in true religious experience is the sense of awe and wonder when humans are confronted by God's majesty as revealed in the universe.

Judaism, it has often been said, is a reasonable faith, no doubt very true, but this must not be taken to mean that there is no room in Judaism for the many things in heaven and earth undreamed of in philosophy. Does not the Jewish tradition speak of the 'secrets of the Torah' still to be revealed?

And there are two hand-breadths in the grasp of Moses. That means that there is a regimen of religious practice, a code of Jewish conduct, a demand of Jewish faith and trust, well within the reach of normal men and women for the enrichment of their spiritual lives. 'The Torah was not given to the ministering angels.' The precepts of the Torah are not the province of an esoteric company of saints. They are the heritage of the congregation of Jacob; standards of good living for men and women of flesh and blood who belong in the world and partake of its pleasures, which they rightly see as God-given. The Torah does not demand that which is impossible for normal persons.

Yet there is a whole range of Jewish experience which belongs neither to the unfathomable nor to the easily acquired. This is represented by the two hand-breadths in the middle. It is within this range that the religious life of human beings is elevated from the realm of the prosaic, the mundane and commonplace, into a glorious faith which calls forth only the best and the highest. In Jewish teaching this aspect is represented by the idea of going beyond the letter of the law in obedience to the higher law of the heart.

Unless Judaism is to become a pedestrian faith, it needs men and women of heroic stature who try to reach out for the divine. While Judaism never despises those whose faith is written only in prose, its finest followers write their life story in poetry. For while part of the Torah must always remain in the hands of God and another part of it in the grasp of all, it is from 'the two hand-breadths in the middle' that human beings receive the beams of glory that make their faces glow.

23

Veyakhel

*And Moses assembled all the congregation of the children of
Israel*   (Exodus 35:1)

The traditional term for a congregation of Jews is *Kehillah
kedoshah*,'holy congregation'. On the face of it, there appears something absurd about using the adjective 'holy' of a company com-
posed of ordinary people with no particular elevated spiritual ambitions and certainly with neither saintly nor mystical pretensions.

The members of a synagogue today sometimes like to refer to
their congregation as an active, successful, resourceful, generous
or forward-looking group. However, were it not for the tradition,
which assembly of Jews would dare to call itself 'holy'?

The answer appears to be that the genius of Judaism seeks to
make us aware that in the values realized by a group of people,
who band together for the common aim of worship and service, a
degree of sanctity is to be found that would be quite beyond their
reach as individuals.

There are three ways in particular in which the congregation is
much more than the individuals of which it is comprised. First, the
members help one another by bringing to the common pool their
gifts of hand, mind and heart as well as assisting one another in
more direct fashion.

Second, it is impossible for men and women to work together
fruitfully and successfully for a common aim without learning the
lesson of co-operation and dialogue. Each person in a community
has a point of view to express which may get on the nerves of
others but which must be treated with respect, difficult though
that may be. In this way, selfish motives are transcended.

Third, with regard to a Jewish congregation, the lives of the members become linked with the glories of the Jewish past and they share the hopes for the future. Their lives become endowed with a new kind of significance. Beautiful and ennobling ceremonies redeem with spiritual poetry what would otherwise have been a drab existence. Most of all, perhaps, man's greatest need, the need to be used in the service of the highest, finds its satisfaction.

Maimonides observes that according to Jewish law anything belonging to the Temple is sacred so that, in Temple times, a trespass offering had to be brought if one used it for a profane purpose. In itself, says Maimonides, it is only a stone or a brick and yet because God's name is attached to it, it becomes holy.

So it is with a Jewish congregation. Looking upon itself as of no intrinsic significance, it cannot fail to appreciate that for all its faults and failings, for all its shortcomings and inadequacies, it is dedicated to the service of the Most High. It can, therefore, lay claim to the tremendous title of 'holy', to which its members must then seek to approximate collectively to the best of their ability. Even of the angels, the prophet tells us that it is only when they call one to the other that they can proclaim: 'Holy, holy, holy'.

> *And all the wise men, that wrought all the work of the sanctuary, came every man from his work which they wrought.* (Exodus 36: 4)

The Talmudic teacher, Levi, noting that Scripture does not say 'every man from *the* work which they made' but 'from his work', said that each craftsman had his own particular task to perform and that no man did the work of his neighbour. For a sanctuary cannot be erected by a company of robots performing a series of mechanical tasks but by creative artists each with his or her special aptitudes and talents.

No great effort of the imagination is required to make this yield the thought that no Jew is expendable in the task of erecting the sanctuary of Jewish life in our generation. Each Jew has an individual contribution to make. So far as God can be said to need any Jew, He needs every Jew.

This view is basic to Judaism. Judaism encourages us to admire and praise the great and good, but it insists that no man can claim absolute superiority over his fellows because of his mental ability, his wealth, his virtues or his achievements. Judaism, unlike other religious faiths, centres on a *people*, not on a *person*. Christianity cannot be imagined without its founder, there can be no Buddhism without Buddha. The Muslim says that not only Allah is God but that Mohammed is his prophet.

Judaism, on the other hand, is not the religion of Moses or Abraham; it is the religion of the children of Israel, of the Jewish people as a whole. The Rabbis could say that if the Torah had not been given through Moses, it could have been given with the same effect through Ezra. There are many great figures in Judaism's long history, from Abraham, Moses, Isaiah, Rabbi Akiba, Maimonides, the Baal Shem Tov, the Vilna Gaon – the list is endless; but each of these is only a link in the chain – a very strong link, but a link none the less – and we, too, are links in the same golden chain.

The wisdom of our ancient teachers speaks to us across the centuries to men and women of the machine age, the age of the computer and the web site, of the huge conglomerates, an age in which the individual is either ignored or rendered insignificant: 'God needs *you*. You are unique. No one has ever lived and no one will ever live, who can think your thoughts and lead your life. So be of good courage and live worthily so that in your own way *you* recognize God's truth and help to fulfil God's purpose.'

24

Pikkudey

And Moses saw all the work, and behold they had done it.
(Exodus 39: 43)

The idea is found in Rabbinic sources that the Tabernacle represents the universe in miniature. God creates the world as His
abode; the place in which His transcendent glory becomes manifest. And human beings return the compliment, as it were, by
building a house to His glory.

This Rabbinic insight is hinted at, too, in the Torah, where the
very vocabulary is the same when used of the creation of the world
and the completion of the Tabernacle. Our verse, for instance, is
obviously paralleled by the verse in the Creation narrative
(Genesis 1:31): 'And God saw everything that He had, and, behold,
it was very good.'

After declaring that each detail of the creation was good, the
Torah states that the creation as a whole was 'very good'. After sur-
veying each detail of the Tabernacle, Moses pronounces the work
good as a whole.

A great artist is concerned with two aspects of his creation. All
the details are executed with skill, each a thing of beauty in itself,
but the details must be balanced adequately in the composition as
a whole.

From the artistic point of view, the whole is more than the sum
of its constituent parts. It is only when the parts are harmoniously
co-ordinated that the artist, and those who admire his composition, can declare themselves satisfied and the work completed.

This is true of the artist of life. Judaism sets much store on detail,
on the right way of carrying out the precepts; but too much preoccupation with detail can result in imbalance. Rabbi Jacob Joseph

of Pulonnoye, chief disciple of the Baal Shem Tov, writing of the principles of Hasidism, scandalized the traditionalist Rabbis when he wrote that one should not be over-scrupulous in attention to detail. The Rabbis were shocked. The whole Rabbinic edifice is founded on attention to the right and wrong way of carrying out the precepts. Presumably the master's intention was not to denigrate the need to serve God through the little things, but only to emphasize that attention to the details should not obscure the vision as a whole.

The broad principles of justice, righteousness, compassion and holiness are to be achieved through the detailed observances of Judaism. However, just as the principles have to be impressed on the daily life of the Jew, the details of that life have to be infused by the principles. Only then can Jewish life be pronounced 'very good'.

PART FOUR
LEVITICUS/*VAYIKRA*

25

Vayikra

Traditionally, the opening word of the *sidra, vayikra*, meaning 'and He called', is written in the Sefer Torah and printed in the Humash with a small *alef* at the end of the word, giving rise to a host of ingenious interpretations.

The Zohar, for instance, states that, since God's call to Moses was outside the Holy Land, it was less powerfully heard. The Midrash, on the other hand, sees the small *alef* as a token of Moses' humility. Moses, on this view, was obliged to write that God called to him, since that was what God had told him to write, but, in his humility. Moses wrote the word with a small *alef* in order not to demonstrate too overtly that he had received the divine call.

Moreover, without the *alef* at the end, the word can be read as *vayikar*, 'and He happened'. By writing the word with a small *alef*, Moses implied that God had had no more than, so to speak, a casual encounter with him.

The nineteenth-century, Italian Bible commentator, Samuel David Luzzatto, provides an entirely adequate explanation for the small *alef* – as well as for practically every other small letter in the Torah. He notes that in almost every instance of a small letter, the same letter appears adjacent to it in the line. It is all too easy for a scribe, when proposing to wrote a letter twice, one after the other in the same line, to omit one of them. In that event, when reading over the line and noticing the omission, he may find that he has no room for the missing letter to be inserted except by squeezing it into the line in a smaller size than the other letters.

Does this mean that the explanation of the Zohar and the Midrash are incorrect? By no means. Even if Luzzatto is right (he is almost certainly) the small letters do appear as such in the Torah, and it is the present form of the Torah into which the ideas are read.

What matters for Judaism is not so much the conjectured, original form, but the form of the living Torah as we have it now. Both textual criticism and Midrashic exposition have their place.

> *When any man of you bringeth an offering unto the Lord.*
> (Leviticus 1:2)

The Rabbis note that the Hebrew words in this verse, if read as they stand, can carry the meaning: 'If any man brings an offering – it shall be his own.' A man must not bring the property of another as his offering to God. Any sacrifice a religious person makes must be his or her own. To give of one's own in the service of God and man is the laudable aim of true religion. To attempt to offer the person and property of someone else is to adopt one of the worse features of idolatrous worship.

There is no sacrificial system in Judaism today, but the lesson contained in the Rabbinic comment of the need to avoid spiritual parasitism is of permanent value. Towards the end of the nineteenth century, the great Lithuanian moralist, Rabbi Israel Salanter, founder of the Musar movement, lay dying, tended by a man paid to look after him. As the end was drawing near, Rabbi Israel observed that the attendant was nervous at the prospect of being left alone with the corpse. Whereupon the dying man spent the last precious moments of his life in reassuring the attendant that it was foolish to be afraid of a lifeless body incapable of doing harm.

For the devout, the last precious moments of life – the hour in which, in the expressive words of the ancient Rabbis, the two worlds kiss – afford a unique experience, when the soul, filled with immortal longings, sheds the garment of the body. Numerous and profound are the stories of how the saints died. It takes a moral giant of the stature of Rabbi Israel to realize that this or any other spiritual experience must not be gained at the sacrifice of the comfort and feelings of other persons. Not to use others for the attainments of our own material advancement is elementary ethics. Rabbi Israel, with much deeper insight, condemned even spiritual advancement at the expense of others, *Man darf nit zein frum auf yenem's plaitzes*, 'one must not use the shoulders of another as stepping stones to piety', was a favourite maxim of Rabbi Israel and his disciples.

To follow this admirable doctrine does not, of course, mean that we must never seek to influence others to share our ideals. Every idealist is concerned to spread his views abroad and wants to see them find a secure place in society. He cannot bring himself to be indifferent to their flouting by those hostile to them or who fail to appreciate their importance. However, it does mean that we must refuse to call upon others to make their contribution unless we, in turn, are willing to make our own.

Not only should we reject the attitude of those who 'compound for sins they are inclin'd to by damning those they have no mind to', but we should cultivate the habit of constantly making more severe demands on ourselves than we make on other people. This idea has been elevated in a great principle of later Rabbinic decision – making that a rabbi, in his religious decisions, should endeavour to interpret the law, whenever possible, in a lenient manner for others and in a strict manner for himself.

The lesson for our day is clear. The world needs its reformers and improvers – without these, progress would be impossible – but, in order for them to succeed in what they do, their greatest efforts and best talents must be directed to that aim which can alone truly convince – the betterment of their own characters, and the improvement of their own selves.

> *No meal-offering, which ye shall bring unto the Lord, shall*
> *be made with leaven; for ye shall make no leaven, nor any*
> *honey, smoke as an offering made by fire unto the Lord.*
> (Leviticus 2:11)

The meal-offering brought to the sanctuary was not to contain leaven or honey. The human palate has a fondness for both the sweet and the sour. It was natural, therefore, for primitive man to put yeast and honey in his meal-offering. He knew that he liked his own food seasoned in this way and he argued that his gods would have the same preferences. As Maimonides writes when discussing this law, the idolaters used to offer yeast and honey to their gods, therefore the Torah prohibits the use of these ingredients for the meal-offering in the Temple. For the aim of the Torah is to eradicate idolatrous worship and to bring men to the service of the true God.

We no longer bring meal-offerings to a Temple, and yet the idea behind this ancient prohibition can be translated most effectively into the idiom of our day. The excessively sour and the excessively sweet are out of place in our Judaism. To capture our hearts and our minds it must be presented neither as a harsh religion, which thwarts all our needs and desires, nor as a sugary, sentimental faith which indulges us too much. Neither a 'yeast' nor a 'honey' religious approach is acceptable.

The religion that is full of sourness, the harsh, intolerant, life-hating, denying religion, how much harm has it done; how many lives have been embittered by religion in over-stern accents! How often do we hear the complaint of people who were turned off Judaism by the sombre and oppressive attitude of their parents towards the Jewish religion! Parents who castigate their young children for innocent pursuits and even for less-innocent ones with severe rebukes encourage in the children the association of religion with everything that is distasteful. For some religious people, faith demands that all the brilliant colours be washed out of life's picture, leaving everything drab and grey. There are some religious people who can feel superior to others only by punishing themselves in the name of their faith. Such people know nothing of what the Rabbis call: 'the joy of the *mitzvah*', that is, the sheer delight of doing God's will.

Life's struggles are hard enough without religion adding to the burden. A consequential faith ought to enable a man to face his problems and help him come to grips with life; ought to teach him how to rejoice in his portion, as the Rabbis say. The meal-offering of Judaism ought not to contain yeast.

So far what has been said is acceptable to most thoughtful people; but it cannot be left at that. For if excessive harshness is harmful in the religious life, excessive and over-flavoured religion is no less harmful. Honey as well as yeast is not acceptable on God's altar. Jews need a religion that presents them with a real challenge, not one which assures them that all is well when it is not. True religious faith is never a mere palliative nor is it a sentimental attachment to the ways of the fathers or to ethnic attraction. It is no 'Fiddler on the Roof' type of nostalgia for the ghetto and ghetto life.

Our text tells us that while no yeast and no honey were to be contained in the meal-offering, the offering had to contain salt. For, to quote Maimonides again, the idolaters never included salt in their offerings. Life worthily lived is not a life of extremes or excesses; but unless religious faith is much more than emotionalism, it will be seasoned with salt, signifying that life is grim but can be a stirring adventure.

26

Tzav

In the book of Exodus we read that Moses broke the tablets of stone containing the word of God when he saw that the people he had led from Egypt had danced before the golden calf. The Midrash asks: Who authorized Moses to break the tablets given to him by God? What right had Moses to cast them from his hands? One of the answers given by the Midrash is of relevance to the religious problems of contemporary Jews. The Midrash suggests that Moses did not, in fact, carry the massive tablets since they were so huge that no human being could possibly carry them down the mountain. Moses found, according to the Midrash, than no sooner had he put his shoulder to the tablets than the tablets carried him, avoiding the yawning crevices and jagged rocks in miraculous fashion; but the tablets possessed this miraculous quality only by virtue of the fact that the power was in the words engraved on them by the finger of God. When the people worshipped the golden calf and danced before it, when they so blatantly disobeyed the word of God on the tablets, the tablets lost their miraculous power to carry Moses. The tablets became immense blocks of lifeless stone and Moses perforce could no longer carry them nor could they carry him. Moses had to let the tablets slip out of his hands.

One of the great questions Jews ask nowadays concerns the role of ritual in Jewish life. How do the rituals in which Judaism abounds make for the service of God? This theme is particularly worth discussing in a comment on this week's *sidra* which is all about the sacrifices and other rites carried out by the priests when they were dedicated.

Every Jew knows that the traditional Jewish Law, the Halakhah, seeks to encompass the whole of life and that this is a significant feature of Judaism; even those who reject this or that detail of the Halakhah appreciate that a non-Halakhic Judaism is bound to be a distortion of the Jewish religion. Critics of the Halakhah can dwell on what they imagine to be the dead hand of the Law, which they contrast with its spirit. But they are ignorant of the life-enhancing quality of the Law. In the Halakhah, Judaism seeks to give concrete expression to the yearning of the spirit. The dedication of the priests has to be carried out in the proper manner because the rituals have to be brought down, so to speak, from heaven to earth. A mere declaration that the Sanctuary is holy and the priests who minister therein are holy would all have been vague and totally unimpressive. As the Midrash puts it, it is not Moses who carries the tablets; the tablets carry Moses.

No religion can achieve anything without its rituals, without the discipline these afford. It is folly to imagine that religious ideas and ideals can flourish in a vacuum. They have to be nourished and sustained by regular practices and detailed regulations. A man may believe that God is the Creator of all and that our lives are in His hand but the Jew who keeps the Sabbath week by week makes this belief a reality in his life. Tagore's wonderful illustration of the violin string is germane to the issue. 'I have on my table' Tagore writes, 'a violin string. It is free to move. I can turn it this way and that way. It is free, but it cannot sing. And then I take it and fix it in my violin. It is no longer free to move in any direction I choose. It is no longer completely free. But it is, for the first time, free to sing.' However, if we are to understand the problem today we cannot just leave it at that. Important though the Halakhah is, it loses its power to inspire if it is all carried out in a mechanical fashion. A book I read years ago contained an amusing printer's error. The printer had, inadvertently, changed the author's 'the ritual of Judaism' into 'the rutual of Judaism'. Ritual or rutual, that is the question. Shall the Halakhah be the spiritual force it was meant to be or will it be allowed to become no more than a soulless routine? The Midrash quoted above reminds us that when the spirit had fled, that when the people surrendered themselves to frenzied, undisciplined dancing before the golden calf, the tablets became no more than heavy stones that even a Moses could not carry.

A stodgy, uninspiring schoolteacher applied for the job of headmaster of an important school, but was passed over. He protested that he had had twenty-five years of experience as a teacher. 'No,' he was told, 'you have one year's experience twenty-five times!'

For Jewish rituals to be vital, new life must infuse them. 'Each day consider the words of the Torah as if they had just been given,' say the Rabbis. We do not obey the dictates of the Halakhah and follow its rituals simply because our ancestors did. They give expression to eternal truths if only we allow them so to do.

27

Shemini

And Moses diligently inquired. (Leviticus 10:16)

The Hebrew for this is *darosh darash*, the second of these words, according to the Masoretic tradition, being the beginning of exactly the second half of the Torah by word division.

For this reason, the rule is that the word *darosh* is the last word of the column in the Sefer Torah, and the word *darash* is the first word of the next column.

So careful were the ancients in establishing completely accurate texts of the Torah that they counted every single word and letter in order to arrive at this kind of conclusion. Elsewhere the marginal note calls attention to the middle letter of the Torah and to the second half of the Torah according to the verse division.

It is a felicitous coincidence that the last word of the first half of the Torah (in the word division) is *darosh* and the first word of the second half of the Torah *darash*, both words forming the expression *darosh darash*, 'diligently inquired'.

Coincidental though it is, there is here a whole philosophy of Judaism. At the heart of the Torah is the idea that the revealed word of God is far more than appears on the surface. Diligent inquiry for the purpose of deeper understanding and ever-fresh application of the message is not optional but is of the essence of the living Torah. To this is devoted the whole of the Midrashic literature.

The very word Midrash denotes inquiry, searching, searching for the truth, studying the inner meaning of the Biblical texts and their further application to life. The word *midrash* is, in fact, derived from the same root, *darash*, 'to inquire'.

Scholars have debated whether teachings derived by the Midrashic method were known (by tradition) independently of the text (the Midrash then being no more than an attempt to read the idea into the text) or whether the derivation is a real one. It seems probable that both methods were used.

Be that as it may, the Midrashic process has continued throughout the history of Torah exposition and it continues today; the original word of God making its impact on Jewish life through the dedicated efforts of those who, like Moses, 'diligently inquired'.

To search for the meaning of the Torah is itself what is meant by the Torah. When Jewish teachers study the Torah, it is not only in order to know what was said long ago, but, more significantly, what is being said to Jews now.

> *These are the living things which ye may eat among all the*
> *beasts that are on the earth.*   (Leviticus 11:2)

Why should Jews obey the dietary laws? This is no new question. Among the many reasons given, the one often advanced today is that they promote health. It is not difficult to account for the popularity of the hygienic interpretation in our day. In response to the challenge of materialistic philosophies, many religious people feel that they can best serve the cause of Judaism by dwelling on the material advantages to be gained by loyalty to Jewish observance. Thus statistics are judiciously selected to prove the immunity of Jews from certain diseases, and it is fondly imagined that this will encourage more and more Jews to keep *kashrut*.

The motives of these worthy people are above suspicion, but the service they render to Judaism is questionable; and there is much that is psychologically unsound and a good deal morally reprehensible. Pychologically unsound, because it is extremely problematical whether people will give up long-established habits on grounds of health, especially if the evidence is somewhat equivocal. The statistics on the correlation of smoking and cancer ought to convince us of this.

The hygienic approach to *kashrut* is morally reprehensible on two grounds. The first is that it implies that Judaism is concerned with the heath and physical well-being of Jews alone and has no interest in that of non-Jews. The Torah positively enjoins that non-kosher meat should be sold to non-Jews (Deuteronomy 14:21).

Second, it is a peculiar way of meeting the challenge of materialism to import this into our religious faith.

All the stress on the physical well-being which results from carrying out religious duties is hardly calculated to fire the imagination. It is all so very prosaic and dull, as inspiring as a Ministry of Health report. Not that health is unimportant. Judaism is a religion of life and Jews cannot believe that its laws are injurious to health. It may well be that the *effect* of *kashrut* observance has been of benefit to health; but there is all the difference in the world between noting this effect and elevating this into the motive or reason for observance.

The hygienic interpretation finds no support in Biblical texts. The keynote in these texts is holiness. The Torah makes no promise of immediate physical pleasure or benefit as the reward for observance of the laws. These laws, the Torah suggests, are difficult to keep. They require much disciplining of the instincts but that is what holiness involves, that human beings learn to subordinate material and physical interests to integrity and principle.

We do a disservice to Judaism if, by superficial 'explanations', we leave it open to a charge of materialism. This is what the foes of Judaism have been saying for centuries, that Jews are materialists even in their religion. Let us not play into their hands by interpretations of the faith without warrant in historic Judaism.

Our ancestors gave their lives for these and similar laws, with no thought of immediate reward, for there is something divine in man which urges him to give of himself unstintingly in the service of his Maker. The truly religious person asks not so much: what can I get out of my religion?' as: 'How can my religion help me to serve God?'

In a world where the ideal of holiness is becoming increasingly valued as the significant element in true religion, Jews should value more and more the lesson of the dietary laws aids to holiness.

28

Tazria

*And the leper in whom the plague is, his clothes shall be
rent, and the hair of his head shall go loose, and he shall
cover his upper lip, and he shall cry: 'Unclean, unclean'.
All the days in which the plague is in him he shall be
unclean; he is unclean; he shall dwell alone; without the
camp shall his dwelling be.* (Leviticus 13:45–6)

In this and the next *sidra* the rules are found of the strange afflic-
tion usually translated in English as 'leprosy' and the one who suf-
fers from it as a 'leper'. There is no need here to consider what
exactly the particular plague or disease actually means but rather
consider the homiletical treatment by the Rabbis, who read the
word for the 'leper', *metzora*, as *motzi shem ra*, 'one who brings out
an evil report', that is, one who seeks to destroy the character of
another person by talking evil of him. According to this Rabbinic
interpretation, the terrible manifestation is visited upon the person
who goes around slandering others so that he will be obliged to be
separated from the community until he is cured. He promoted
strife and hatred and thus caused friction in his society and he has
to be apart from society until he learns his lesson. Obviously the
Rabbis were thinking of the evils of slander in their own day. They
were preaching against what has been known ever since in Jewish
teaching as *lashon hara*, 'the evil tongue'. When Israel Meir Kagan
(1838–1933) observed, in his native Lithuania, how private and
social life was disintegrating as a result of character assassination,
he resolved to write and publish a book in which he describes in
detail the rules governing *lashon hara*. He called the book *Hafetz
Hayyim*, after the verses in Psalms (34:12–13): 'Who is he who
delighteth in life [*hehafetz hayyim*] and loveth many days that he

may see good. Keep thy tongue from evil, and thy lips from speaking guile.' After this work, the author became known throughout Jewry as 'the Hafetz Hayyim', and a saintly leader of world renown. In Yeshivah circles to this day the work is studied assiduously.

The work *Hafetz Hayyim* purports to be a Halakhic compendium, in which the rules and regulations regarding *lashon hara* are presented, in legal style, as if the book is discussing, for example, which food is kosher and which not. Whether the Halakhic approach is applicable to such matters is another matter. Critics of the work (and the Hafetz Hayyim himself tries to meet the objection) have noted that the vast majority of the Rabbinic statements on the subject belong to the more flexible Aggadah than the precise Halakhah. For instance, there are numerous rabbinical teachings against anger and flying into a temper, but one can hardly look up in a Code of Jewish law when it is justified to lose one's tempe and when not. In any event, the Rabbinic homilies on the *metzora*, while belonging to the Aggadah, have been taken very seriously by devout Jews, common sense generally operating in complex situations.

For instance, would investigative journalism be allowed according to Jewish law? It would probably be better to formulate this as: 'Would investigative journalism be allowed according to Jewish ethics?' It is difficult to find actual passages in the Bible or the Talmud about this question, since there was no investigative journalism in ancient times. There was no such thing as journalism. What can be extrapolated from the sources is that the dissemination of material calculated to harm others should not be perpetrated and in many circumstances it falls under the heading of the severely condemned *lashon hara*. However, whether where the exposure of crooked dealing or the lowering of moral standards by people in power is beneficial to society, has to be weighed up by the journalist's conscience.

In the Talmudic period the majority of the laws of *tzaraat* were of no practical consequence. Yet the Talmudic Rabbis discussed the Halakhah of 'plagues', *negaim*, as they did all the other laws of the Torah. A whole tractate of the Mishnah is devoted to the subject as well as numerous passages in the rest of the Talmud. The rules of *negaim* were considered to be among the more difficult subjects of study. When the great Rabbi Akiba expressed a particularly daring view in matters of Aggadah, his colleagues said to him in so many words, do not bother yourself with Aggadah. This not your forte. Study instead, put your brilliant mind to the study of *negaim*. The result of this was a division between the rules of *negaim* and the typical homiletical ideas mentioned at the beginning of this comment.

Although, generally speaking, Maimonides was the great rationalist among the medieval Jewish philosophers, when he came to discuss *tzaraat* he sees no way of explaining the whole phenomenon other than by invoking the supernatural. According to Maimonides, the sinner, the slanderer, as above, is given a stern warning by a supernatural manifestation appearing on the walls of his house. If he takes the warning and desists from his evil conduct, the plague spot will disappear. If not, a further warning is given by the plague spot appearing on his garments. Finally, the plague spot appears on his body. Rationalist though he was, Maimonides evidently felt that it is better not to be too rationalistic in an area in which rationalism is powerless to help.

29

Metzora

... cedar wood, and scarlet, and hyssop. (Leviticus 14:4)

The Rabbis were adept at turning the most unpromising material to good homiletical account. From the apparently dry, uninspiring details of the purification rites they derive the lesson that over-weening pride is the source of contamination and sin, and that the cultivation of a humble spirit is the first step towards regeneration.

The mighty cedar is the loftiest of trees, the hyssop the lowliest of bushes. The scarlet dye is in Hebrew *tolaat*, referring to the worm from which the dye is manufactured. Thus the three ingredients in the purification rite are used by the Rabbis to hint at pride and its remedy, humility. The sinner, puffed up with pride, elevated like the cedar, must learn to abase himself, to be humble as the hyssop and the worm are lowly among created things. The Psalmist's anguished cry (Psalms 22:7): 'But I am a worm and no man,' is something more than mere Oriental hyperbole.

This is hardly popular doctrine. Nietzsche's vehement attack on self-abasement is but an extreme version of what many accept. 'If you think of yourself as a worm do not be surprised if people tread on you', the self-assertive maintain. And yet pride is generally recognized as the cause of much evil, the cause of unrest, envy and bitterness in the lives of individuals and the cause of aggression, cruelty and bloody wars in the life of nations.

Not that humility, not as a mere opposite of pride but a shining virtue, is easily attained. All the moralists speak from experience when they maintain how difficult it is to eradicate pride from the human heart. Moses Haim Luzzatto, author of one of the great texts of Jewish saintliness, *Mesilat Yesharim*, 'Path of the Upright', was so convinced that only the man of complete honesty and integrity can achieve true humility that he placed this virtue on the highest rung of the ladder of saintliness. This author, with keen psychological insight, delineates the subtle forms a spurious humility takes. It is not only, the obviously vain and conceited, he says, who suffer from pride. There is the person who feels so superior to others that he can cheerfully forgo their marks of respect. There is the man who prides himself on his humility, who imagines that he has all the virtues including humility; and there is the man, conscious of false humility, who is proud that he has none of this. The worm is not only proud and puffed up when it imagines itself to be a cedar, but even more so when it takes pride in being a worm.

How then can pride be overcome? The great Nahmanides gives the answer in a letter to his son, whom he advises to acquire the habit of thinking of every man as his superior. 'If the man you meet,' this sage writes, 'is clearly your better in learning, in character, or in achievement, there is no room for pride. But even if you are superior to him in these things, reflect that your responsibilities are thereby the greater. God has been more lavish in His gifts to you and more is demanded of you. For all you know to the contrary, he may be fulfilling his function in life far more worthily than you are fulfilling yours.'

Not everyone would be prepared to follow Nahmanides' prescription and one can feel sorry for the poor son. Yet it remains true that the man who has conquered pride has banished from his life some of its torments and the frustrations of burning but unsatisfied ambitions. His life is not poisoned by consuming envy at the successes of others. Perhaps no one can ever achieve true humility – it might even be argued that to try to do so is itself the worst kind of pride – but the nearer we get to the ideal the greater our reward not only in the Hereafter but even now in our life on earth.

For the man free from pride and the envy which stems from pride has the whole world for his province. He alone can enjoy fully the good things of life, for there is nothing to turn them sour in his mouth. It remains literally true that 'the meek shall inherit the earth'.

30

Aharey Mot

After the doings of the land of Egypt, wherein ye dwelt, shall ye not do; and after the doings of the land of Canaan, whither I bring you, shall ye not do; neither shall ye walk in their statutes. (Leviticus 18:3)

The Hebrew of 'neither shall ye walk in their statutes' is *uvehukkotehem lo telekhu*. In the next *sidra* the verse occurs: 'And ye shall not walk in the customs of the nation, which I am casting out before you' (Leviticus 20:23).The Hebrew, rendered in the English version as 'the customs of the nation', is *behukkot ha-goy*. Thus, in the context, the term *hukkot ha-goy* refers to the practices or customs of the Egyptians and the Canaanites and seems to denote the sexual immoralities of these nations; but from Talmudic times and onwards *hukkot ha-goy* denotes practices peculiar to other religions. The Jew is expected to avoid conduct or dress pertaining to the followers of a religion other than Judaism.

This concept of *hukkot ha-goy* has always been somewhat uncertain of application. The implications of the Biblical passages are that the stern warning was originally intended against sexual irregularities which must be rejected by the holy nation. Hence an early Rabbinic Midrash comments that the verse does not forbid Jews to copy Gentile architectural styles since this is purely a matter of convention and convenience and of no doctrinal significance.

As the law developed and as Jews lived in many diverse lands, each with its own customs, considerable latitude was allowed in this whole area. Provided a practice was universal among human beings, or had no close association with religious or superstitious ideas, even if peculiar to a particular people, it did not fall under the heading of *hukkot ha-goy*.

In the grey area, the line between what is permitted and what is forbidden is finely drawn by the good taste and sense of discrimination of the Jewish community.

Thus synagogues have been built in Christian lands in the Gothic style, but obviously never in the cruciform mode, or with a tower and spire, like a church. The fifteenth-century sage, Rabbi Joseph Colon, permitted a Jewish physician to wear the special robe worn by Gentile doctors, since this was no more than an indication of his profession. Whether this ruling can be extended to Rabbis and cantors wearing canonicals is rather more debatable. Some Orthodox Rabbis have frowned on the wearing of canonicals or a clerical collar, but in Anglo-Jewry until fairly recently Rabbi Colon's ruling was extended to permit these. True, it used to be argued, these modes of dress have been copied from the practices of the Anglican Church, but they are not like a cross, which has doctrinal significance, but merely a means of adopting the clergyman's professional garb.

It follows from all this that customs which have a pagan origin, or which have decidedly Christian associations, should not be adopted by Jews – one should not have, for example, Halloween parties or 'Hanukkah trees'.

The Hebrew titles of this *sidra* and the two that follow are: *Aharey Mot, Kedoshim, and Emor.* These words can, without too much distortion, be read to mean: 'Speak only holy of the dead' and have been so rendered in a well-known Jewish saying, the equivalent of the Latin tag: *de mortuis nil nisi bonum.* There is generally ripe wisdom in folk sayings that have stood the test of time. It may be worthwhile to to examine this apophthegm in greater detail.

Why have peoples, both ancient and modern, considered it wrong to speak ill of the dead? Partly, because of man's reverence for the mystery of life and death and the gulf dividing the two. The dead belong to another world. Their labours over, they can enjoy none of this life's pleasures and taste none of its sorrows.

The attitude of the living towards the dead is a curious compound of awe and pity upon which it would be sacrilege to obtrude with words of calumny. Present also is the element of superstition, fear of what the dead might do if they were wronged. But of this the famed Hafetz Hayyim, whose whole life was devoted to combating the evils of malicious slander, rightly observed that, contrary to the popular view, it is a far more serious offence to speak ill of the living who can be harmed by our words than of the dead who are beyond our power to victimize.

However there is more to this than refusing to speak ill of the dead because it is forbidden. The truth is that generally we have no desire to speak badly of those who have passed away. Why do people take delight in running down others? Is it not because by this means their own worth is bolstered up? Conscious of their own inferiority, as all men are at one time or another, they gain security by being able to show, to themselves as well as to others, 'Bad I am but, at least, I did not do *that.*' But the dead are not our rivals. They cannot occupy positions we would like to hold. We can bask in their reflected glory, without feeling that its light tends to obscure our own. Slander of the dead, because it holds out very little promise of self-assurance, possesses few attractions.

There is an important lesson in all this. Only rid a man of his feelings of inferiority and insecurity and he will have no need to remove others from the throne of honour in order to seat himself safely upon it. Said the Baal Shem Tov: *The Lord will give strength unto His people; the Lord will bless His people with peace,* for the strong of soul can happily endure the successes of others.

How is this strength to be acquired? While in no way detracting from the many positive achievements of modern psychiatry in helping to produce the type of personality that is called 'well-integrated', the real source of this strength, as the verse reminds us, is a sound religious faith. The man of real faith learns to understand that the gifts, material and spiritual, with which men are endowed are God-given. He recognizes the futility of trying to encroach on the preserves of another and thus attempting to frustrate God's plan for each of His children. The man of faith knows with Emerson that 'talents differ, all is well and wisely put'. His reward is serenity of soul. It is the Lord who gives strength to His people. It is the Lord who blesses them with peace.

—31—

Kedoshim

Love thy neighbour. (Leviticus 19: 18)

This verse, the 'golden rule', is generally interpreted as a *command* to love one's neighbour. But how can you command love? You can command a man to *do* something; you cannot command him to feel something in his heart. The essence of love is its spontaneity. The emotions cannot be turned on like a tap. If a man already loves his neighbour, no command is necessary. If he does not, no command can be effective. A command to love reminds us of nothing so much as those old prayer books with detailed instructions in Yiddish: 'Here one must weep bitterly'; 'At this stage the heart must be full of joy'. A famous Jewish classic, dealing with such precepts as 'Love thy neighbour', is entitled: 'Duties of the heart'; but this is precisely the difficulty – how can there be *duties* of the heart?

Jewish tradition, it would seem, has two answers to this question: one, if it may be put this way, on the lower level of religious experience, the other on the higher level. The first answer would be that the golden rule is not, in fact, an appeal to the emotions but a challenging call to action. It is frequently overlooked that the full text of the verse in which the rule is contained runs as follows:

> *Thou shalt not take any vengeance, nor bear any grudge against the children of thy people, but thou shalt love thy neighbour as thyself: I am the Lord.* (Leviticus 19:18)

That is to say, the rule can be paraphrased as: 'Love your neighbour as yourself so that you do not do unto him that which you would not want him to do unto you. Therefore, do not take revenge or bear any grudge against him.' It is well known that, according to the Talmud, the great sage Hillel gave this kind of paraphrase to the Gentile who asked to be taught the whole of the Torah in a single maxim. Seen in this light the emphasis is not on the emotions but on the *deed*.

This, however, is no more than the minimum requirement of the Jewish ethic. This is the standard at which every Jew must aim; but Jewish teaching knows too of the higher sense in which the golden rule is an appeal to the heart, of the often severe demands made upon those who would tread the difficult and risky road to self-perfection. And in reply to the question if love can be ordered, it would reply that the command is for love to be so cultivated that it becomes second nature. The paradox here, as a prominent nineteenth-century Jewish moralist said, is that the precept is not fulfilled until one is unaware that a precept is being fulfilled. The love of one's neighbour must become a spontaneous reaction. To be consciously aware that one is carrying out a *mitzvah* when loving one's neighbour is to sacrifice the essence of that very *mitzvah*.

How can this love be cultivated? One of the ways is by constant obedience to the golden rule in the first sense mentioned. Judaism believes in the healing power of action, hence the emphasis on the Halakhah, the legal side of the religion. By doing things in obedience to lofty ideals, we bring those ideals down from heaven, if it is not too precious to say so. The ideals become nearer, more real, we make them our own. By refraining as far as we can from doing harm to others, by practising charity and benevolence, we gradually learn to to express our personality in this way and our character does change for the better. Judaism does not accept the cynical view that you cannot change human nature.

Another method is to reflect deeply on Jewish teachings concerning God and man. A distinction has justifiably been made between loving a person and liking him. When a woman refuses a proposal by saying: 'I am very sorry. I am fond of you but I do not love you', she is not using the word *love* in the sense in which it is used in the golden rule. Obviously, the particular attraction that is the basis of married love, or the special regard of members of a family for each other, cannot be extended to embrace other people. There are, too, people whom we positively dislike for one reason or another and there are people we have never met and know nothing about. We cannot possibly *like* these people but we can *love* them. For the word *ve-ahavta* in our text refers to the sympathy and understanding and the desire for identification with other human beings that results from reflection on such things as our common humanity, that all human beings have the same basic needs, are hurt in the same way and are pleased in the same way, that their happiness is our happiness and their misery our misery. John Donne's words have been quoted too many times to be really effective and in them the poet is perhaps overstating the case, yet there is truth in them:

> Any man's death diminishes me, because I am involved in Mankind, and therefore never send to know for whom the bell tolls: it tolls for thee.

Above all, the way to cultivate the love of one's fellows is to reflect that they are all created in the image of God; that He loves them all and has a place for them in His purpose. It is no coincidence that the verse concludes with the words: 'I am the Lord'. Much has been said on the relationship between religion and ethics. To anyone with open eyes, the facts make it untrue that there can be no sound ethical conduct without religion, that non-religious people cannot be good people in the ethical sense; but ethical monotheism, the religion that is Judaism, elevates ethics on to a different plane. From the theistic standpoint, ethics is far more than a system evolved by society for its survival. The ethical life is a religious imperative because God who gave us life gave it to our fellows, because if it can be said that God needs any man, He needs every man. It was in this spirit that a Hasidic master said: 'Would that I loved the greatest saint as much as God loves the greatest sinner.'

32

Emor

Speak unto the children of Israel saying: In the seventh month, in the first day of the month, shall be a solemn rest untoyou, a memorial proclaimed with the blast of horns, a holy convocation. (Leviticus 23:24)

This is the source for sounding the shofar on the festival of Rosh Hashanah, for which many reasons have been advanced. According to Maimonides, it is the nature of the shofar to rouse the indifferent to a deeper sense of reality, to summon man from the pursuit of shadows. Yet may it not be that the true message of the shofar is to be found as much in the silence which follows the sounding of its notes? The shofar *heralds* the voice of the spirit, but that voice speaks to us out of the resulting stillness. The sound of the shofar must be loud enough to be heard above the din of a strident, noisy world, but its call is to contemplation and inner peace, to the need for effecting a lull in our busy rushing from place to place, so as to take stock of ourselves.

In the well-known festival meditation, God is described sitting on the Throne of Judgement. Among the images found in this meditation is that of the 'great shofar': 'The great trumpet is sounded, the still small voice is heard.' The aim of our prayers on Rosh Hashanah and Yom Kippur is that the still small voice be heard. It is for this that the great trumpet is sounded. It is clear that the author took his theme from the narrative in the book of Kings of Elijah's vision of God. The fiery champion of monotheism, obliged to flee for his life, hears the sound of a great wind, rending the mountains and breaking the rocks in pieces; but God was not in the wind. And after the wind there was an earthquake; but God was not in the earthquake. And after the earthquake there was a fire; but God was not in the fire. And, then, after the fire, there was a still small voice or, as some translate it, a voice of gentle stillness, out of which God spoke to Elijah.

The definition of religion as what a man does with his solitariness is far from perfect, as Judaism understands religion. It fails to take notice of the social aspect of religion, on which Judaism sets great store. Judaism is, too, a religion of action, which offers no encouragement to the idler sitting with folded arms, allowing the world to go by.

There is still, however, much in the definition, that the only way to find a path through the turmoil and chaos of a materialistic world is to listen to God, at times, speaking from the stillness. As the Midrash puts it:

> The giving of the Torah was preceded by thunder and lightning and the almighty sound of the shofar, but when no ox lowed, no bird sang, the Ofanim did not fly, the Serafim uttered not their 'Holy, holy, holy', the sea did not roar, no creature uttered a sound, all listened in breathless silence to the words announced by an echoless voice.

It has been said that there are two kinds of men and women – those who stop and think and those who stop thinking! At the very least, the Days of Awe, Rosh Hashanah and Yom Kippur should be utilized for serious reflection on the good life as understood in Judaism. We should resolve to be not of those who have stopped thinking but of those who think to some purpose.

> *Ye shall dwell in booths seven days: all that are Israelites born shall dwell in booths. That your generations may know that I made the children of Israel to dwell in booths, when I brought them out of the land of Egypt: I am the Lord thy God.* (Leviticus 23:42–4)

It does not require much effort of the imagination to see in the command to dwell in booths on the festival of Sukkot, a reminder to man not to glory in his achievements, but to recognize that it is God who gives man the power to subdue nature to his ends. This is a favourite theme of Jewish preachers on Sukkot. The *sukkah* teaches, the preachers are fond of saying, reliance on the divine. It teaches us not to put our trust in the work of our hands. It teaches us that unless we accept God's sovereignty, our paths are bound to be hindered by obstacles of various kinds. The simple life under God is the message of the *sukkah* or so it is said by the preachers.

And yet to interpret the message of the *sukkah* simply as a 'back to nature' call would be to misunderstand its purpose.

It is no new phenomenon that life in great cities tends to be harsh, grasping and cruel. There is usually a greater attachment to religion in a country village than in large towns. In modern Japan, for instance, it was observed that as the country folk moved into the towns to take their part in the industrialization of their nation, they lost their hold on the religious practices of their ancestral way of life. Western technological methods have spread over the whole world and it is not surprising that many people find the stress and the severe strain of the new life overbearing, depriving man of his happiness, his freedom and his peace of mind.

It is not surprising, therefore, that some thinkers have urged mankind to go back – to go back to the good old days, back to the pre-industrial age, to escape from the domination of the machine, to call a halt to the progress of science. This theory has great fascination for some minds. The trouble is that it cannot work. Having tasted the benefits of progress, men will not willingly forgo them.

What then is the solution? The answer is provided by the *sukkah*, if only man will place his life in the hands of God, if only he will surrender his claims to independence even from his Maker. 'Go out,' the Torah commands the Jew, 'from your proud dwelling and dwell for seven days in the *sukkah* so that when you do return to your home you will come to realize that all your power and wealth and achievements are God's blessing to you and must not be used for unworthy ends.'

The Rabbis refer to the *sukkah* as a casual dwelling. By inhabiting this casual dwelling, the *sukkah*, we acquire a better, a more wholesome perspective, and when we return home after being in the *sukkah*, we bring back with us into our lives the spirit of reliance on God and faith in Him which can alone free us from the tyranny of things, so that nature becomes, as it was meant to be, our servant, not our master. This is the way to joy – Sukkot is the 'season of joy' – the way to peace. We speak of the *sukkah* of peace and in our prayers we pray for the day when God will spread the *sukkah* of His peace over all the inhabitants of earth.

33

Behar

*Speak unto the children of Israel, and say unto them:
When ye come into the land which I give you, then shall
the land keep a sabbath unto the Lord.*   (Leviticus 25:2)

There has been much discussion on how the Sabbatical years are
to be calculated. For instance, there is a Talmudic discussion on
how the fiftieth year, the Jubilee, is to be counted – whether as
apart from the previous and subsequent cycles or whether it is also
the beginning of the next cycle. There were also debates in the
middle ages as to when the count of the Sabbatical years began.
Nevertheless, the tradition affirms which year is the Sabbatical
year in the present era, the year 5761 for example. The law of the
Sabbatical year as laid down in this *sidra* is that during this year the
land of Israel (the law applies only to this land, not outside it) the
fields were not to be cultivated and the year is to be a Sabbath unto
the Lord.

Despite the efforts of prominent Rabbis to provide leniencies in
the law, pious farmers in present-day Israel still observe the
Sabbatical year in all its severity. The official Israeli Rabbinate has,
however, permitted the use of the legal fiction of selling the land to
a non-Jew to whom the law obviously does not apply.

In any event, as our *sidra* states, the land belongs to the Lord in
the sense that the whole institution serves to demonstrate, like the
weekly Sabbath, that humans do not really own their possessions
but are stewards with the need to use their worldly goods in accordance with God's will.

Many years ago there lived a man with very unconventional
views. This man was a shopkeeper whose practice it was to close

his shop to customers one day each year, refusing to sell any of his goods on that day. His reasoning was as follows: 'As a good shop-keeper I am obliged to subscribe to the view that the customer is always right; but I know that the customer is frequently wrong. I have to go along with it but the only way I can preserve my self-respect is to set aside a day on which the customer is always wrong'! No one suggests that the practice of this strange shop-keeper should be followed; but his practice helps us to understand the purpose behind the Sabbatical year. Man is subservient to material things. The farmer toils in his fields to wrest from the soil his daily bread. The Torah commands him to let his fields go untended for one whole year, so that he is reminded that he is the master of nature, not its slave.

All this contains an important lesson for present-day mankind. We are all so absorbed in our efforts to make a living that we are in danger of forgetting how to live; and how much tragedy and suf-fering has been brought upon mankind by national greed, by great powers seeking cynically to enlarge their borders and their sphere of influence. An old Jewish legend tells of a loaf of bread and a stick which came down from heaven tied together. God says: 'If you obey My laws then here is the loaf of bread for you to eat. If you disobey My laws then here is the stick to beat you.' No fantasy this but sober fact. For mankind is given the choice between the loaf of bread and the stick. This earth can support human life. It can bring happiness and blessing to man if only he will have the good sense to see life as God's gift and try to live in the light of God's truth. Of course, the life of mankind is far too complicated for any such neat solutions to be available to his many problems; but the laws of the Sabbatical year, though they do not and cannot provide anything like a blueprint for the creation of a better world, still serve as an ancient reminder of a time when the earth was the Lord's and the fullness thereof.

— 34 —

Behukkotai

> *He shall not inquire whether it be good or bad, neither shall he change it; and if he change it at all, then both it and that for which it is changed shall be holy; it shall not be redeemed.* (Leviticus 27: 33)

A good animal set aside for a sacrifice must not be exchanged for one of inferior quality; nor must an inferior animal be exchanged for a good animal. The first law is intelligible; only the best is good enough as a sacrifice to God. But what reason can there be for prohibiting the exchange of a weak, puny offering for one of better quality?

Maimonides offers this explanation. In a moment of intense religious fervour, the Israelite might set aside the best of his herd as a sacrifice, but doubts may begin to assail him when his ardour gives way to a more sober mood. He may then have misgivings about his excessive generosity. Not wishing, however, to recognize calculating prudence, he may succeed in persuading himself that the inferior animal he intends to offer as a substitute is, in some ways at least, superior to the first. And it is in order to avoid this kind of dissembling that the Torah prohibits any exchange.

A shrewd comment! For how often are people tempted to preserve their self-respect while sacrificing their integrity by allowing their faults to masquerade as virtues. Psychologists call this 'rationalization' and refer to the cigarsmoker who thinks the ash is good for the carpet or the fox-hunter who claims that the fox enjoys the hunt. At a more serious level, men intoxicated by the lust for power have used religion as a cloak with which to cover the most horrible and perverse deeds, not always consciously or cynically, but by allowing themselves to believe that they were serving God when they were really serving the devil.

Some would cite this as evidence that religious faith is false; but it is not religion that is at fault when base men use it to further their own ends. The Rabbis realistically faced this issue when they said that for the virtuous the Torah is a soul-healing balm, but for the vicious the Torah itself becomes a deadly poison.

True religion demands 'truth in the inward parts'. Undoubtedly there are religious people whose faith is little more than an emotional prop, even a means of justifying that which they know deep in their hearts to be wrong; but the faith of a real believer is a powerful searchlight, casting its merciless beams on ignoble motives, exposing them for what they are.

This is why the Freudian accusation that religion is 'wishful thinking' sounds so hollow. A strange sort of wishful thinking to subject one's most intimate thoughts to the incorruptible and ever-vigilant scrutiny of the 'stern daughter of the voice of God'. For Judaism, notwithstanding the refusal to dwell too much, as do other faiths, on the essential sinfulness of human nature, encourages its adherents to pray at all times: 'Purify our hearts to serve Thee in truth.'

PART FIVE
NUMBERS/*BEMIDBAR*

35

Bemidbar

The Book of Numbers is called in Hebrew *bemidbar*, 'In the wilderness', because this word occurs at the beginning of the book and it was the old Jewish practice to adopt one of the opening words of a book for its title. A lesser-known Jewish title is *Humash Ha-Pekkudim* and this is the exact equivalent of 'Numbers', referring to the contents of the book, a large portion of which deals with numbering the people. It was, however, the first title that became the more popular, particularly since all the events recorded in this book do take place in the wilderness.

The 'generation of the wilderness', despite their murmurings and backsliding – which the narrative does not seek to hide – are viewed with a good deal of sympathy in the later tradition. They are referred to in the Midrashic sources as the 'generation of knowledge'. It was they, after all, who witnessed the miracle of the Exodus and to whom God spoke at Sinai.

Why was the Torah given particularly to this generation in the wilderness? The Rabbis pose the question, to which two answers especially stand out for their significance for Jewish life.

The first reason given is that the wilderness belongs to no people but is free for all. Had the Torah been given in the Holy Land, it might have been seen as the exclusive preserve of the people of Israel.

To be sure, the full observance of the Torah is for Jews alone, but there are are man conduct, the Torah for the Gentile world.

Judaism is not a national religion – there is a particularistic aspect of Judaism, but Judaism is also a universalistic faith. Nor is Judaism a mystery religion – like the wilderness in which the Torah was given, its truth is open to all.

Second, to venture out into the unknown with danger lurking

at every step and with no obvious guarantee of success was a tremendous act of faith in God.

The prophet Jeremiah (2:2) proclaims in God's name that He remembers Israel's love and loyalty in its youth in daring the hazards of the wilderness. Perhaps more than any other factor, what has enabled Judaism to survive is the intense loyalty of its adherents ready to follow the divine call wherever it may lead.

A question that has puzzled many intelligent readers of the Bible is why there should be included in the Book of Numbers especially those dreary lists of names. They are, on the surface, about as edifying – as someone has said – as the London Telephone Directory. In a book published many years ago dealing with the English Sunday, as it then was, the boring nature of Church services is attributed partly to the lists of names. The writer suggests that it is as relevant as a similar list in English:

> Smith and Higgins and Webb-Johnson,
> And Strawson and Nichols and Dr Jones,
> Lawrence and Browne and Evans of the
>   family of Evans

What is the answer? Why does Jewish tradition insist on reading these names year by year as part of the *sidra*? We could, of course, say that the Pentateuch, as the source of Judaism, occupies a very special place in the consciousness of the Jew and he, therefore, treats it with the utmost reverence and steadfastly refuses to be selective with regard to the passages he reads. Indeed, the Sefer Torah must contain the whole of the Five Books without any omissions if it is to be regarded as fit for use in the synagogue. Such, at least, is the ruling of the standard Code of Jewish Law, the *Shulhan Arukh*.

Is such a reply sufficient? Are we not justified in seeking a more adequate reason for reading these lists of names? If we think about it we can see that behind all these records there lies a great truth. The truth is this, that each family in ancient times had its own specific contribution to make to the life of the people as a whole and that each individual has a personal role to play in the drama of Jewish history. A careful examination of the early chapters of the Book of Numbers reveals that the Torah subtly suggests that each individual is important in his or her own right. The reiteration of those ancient names is to teach that our individual lives are so many strands in the beautiful tapestry of Jewish life and that if any is missing the total effect is marred. Only God Himself can assess the true quality of an individual life. Human beings are called upon to value each human life, which, as the Rabbis said, is a whole world of its own.

All this should not, of course, result in an attitude of unbridled individualism. Judaism is a social religion, reminding us always that there are wider aims than the cultivation of one's own character and the importance of self-realization. The lesson of the Book of Numbers is that if we are to succeed in helping to create a better and more stable society we must start, though not end, with ourselves.

36

Naso

*...the vow of a Nazirite, to consecrate himself unto the
Lord.* (Numbers 6: 2)

One of the Rabbis taught that the Nazirite, who denies himself
wine, is a holy man. Another Rabbi taught that the Nazirite is a
sinner in denying himself God's gift of wine. Contrary to the
generally accepted view, there is room in the wide range of Jewish
religious expression for ascetic tendencies.

There have been great Jews who have interpreted the call of
religion in world-renouncing terms, who have striven mightily to
subdue the flesh; and there have been others, equally great, who
have preached a life-affirming religion, who looked upon the
pleasures of this world not as snares or temptations but as God's
bounty to His creatures.

Naturally, it is the second view which is popular today. The
modern temper is impatient with the self-tormenting recluse. It
considers his condition to be unhealthy and unwise if not morbid
and pathological. Our age seems to adopt the view of the Rabbi
who declared the Nazirite to be a sinner.

When, however, the modern Jew stresses the life-affirming
aspects of his faith, is he always fully aware of the implications of his
doctrine? He is certainly far off the mark if he interprets the view that
Judaism encourages its adherents to love life as meaning that
Judaism is an easy religion. 'What is to God is to God. What is to man
is to man', may be a comfortable compromise for the half-committed.
It does not correspond to any recognizable version of the ancient
faith. A significant religion demands all or it demands nothing.

The idea that the Nazirite is a sinner is no open door to self-
indulgence. The opposite is the truth. The hermit, the ascetic, the

recluse, cannot see how the ideal life can be lived in an imperfect society. They consequently withdraw from the world in a desperate attempt to preserve undiluted the precious wine of true spirituality.

The other view we do right to embrace looks upon such an attitude as escapism. The world needs the good person and the good person needs the world. There are wrongs to be righted, evils to be overcome, opportunities to help those in need, potentialities for good to be realized, beauty to be created, truth to be sought. In the words of the Zohar, man was created to turn darkness into light, to make the bitter sweet. The Jew, it is implied, must have the courage to go out into the world and participate to the full in the world's work without losing his sense of consecration.

The ministering angels, say the mystics, are called in Scripture 'those who stand still'. Human beings, here on earth, are called 'those who walk'. For only by fighting evil in an imperfect world can there be progress on the road leading to God. If the Nazirite is described as 'consecrated unto God', the good who live valiantly in the world are consecrated to God in an even higher sense. For the King of Kings is best served not by the sweet singer uttering His praises far from the heat of the battle, but by the brave warrior who struggles for His truth to emerge triumphant.

His offering was one silver dish. (Numbers 7:13, 25, 31f.)

When the lengthy tedious list of the gifts that the princes brought to the Sanctuary is read in the synagogue, even the most devout worshipper may be excused an occasional yawn. Scripture seems to have forsaken its usual strict economy in the use of words. Even if for some reason it is necessary for us to know what gifts were presented by the ancient nobles, surely it would have sufficed if we were informed that each of them gave a silver dish weighing five shekels, a silver bowl, a golden dish and so on. Seeing that all the princes brought identical gifts, why the detailed, wearisome reiteration of the complete list, unvaried apart from the donors' names?

The Hafetz Hayyim offered the following solution. He pointed out how remarkable it is that all the princes should have agreed on the amount they were each to contribute. They evidently decided that the cause of the Sanctuary would best be served by a uniform

gift rather than by each attempting to outshine the other in generosity. These ancient Hebrew worthies preferred to honour God
instead of seeking honour for themselves in an undignified contest
for 'one-upmanship': 'You give only one golden dish, I shall do better and give two.'

What a lesson for *kavod* seekers, for those who would use the
opportunities given to them of communal service as means for
advancing their own selfish ambitions! Not that any of us are, or
indeed can be, entirely free from egotistic motives in the good we
do. Even the most saintly and altruistic are pleased when their
efforts on behalf of good causes are recognized. We all need
encouragement and we are entitled, to some extent, to experience
a sense of gratification when our humble efforts to increase in
some measure the happiness and well-being of others does not go
unnoticed. However, there is all the difference in the world
between a sense of pride and achievement *incidental* to our altruistic endeavours and the purposeful self-seeking motive which
impels us to ask in every situation: 'What's in it for me?'

No person who engages in communal work is without some
degree of altruism and none is entirely without a measure of self-
interest. It is all a question of degree. One of the most important
aims of our religious faith is to encourage us to try to approximate
to the ideal of disinterested service. The closer we get to this ideal
the less we shall be affected by slights, real or imagined, that are
the inevitable lot of those who serve a community; the less we
shall be concerned about ourselves and the more for the success of
the cause for which we labour; the less we shall think in terms of
receiving, the more in terms of giving.

Happy indeed is the communal worker and leader who, at the
end of a long and fruitful life of service, can lift up his ten fingers
heavenward and exclaim, as we are told Rabbi Judah the Prince
did: 'It is revealed and known to Thee that I have not tasted of this
world's delights even to the extent of my little finger.' However,
even for us lesser mortals it should be possible to avoid the futile
bickering and selfish manoeuvring for position and power that all
too frequently embitter communal life and spell ruin to many a
good cause.

Read in this light, the ancient list of gifts is no irrelevant inter-
lude in the synagogue service but a potent reminder, of which we
all stand in need, that noble-hearted personalities can respond to
the challenge of their better nature to serve 'for the sake of Heaven'

so that the words Moses is said to have uttered when the work of the Sanctuary was complete can be realized in our own communities: 'May the Shekinah rest on the work of your hands.'

37

Behaalotekha

Make thee two trumpets of silver; of beaten work shalt thou make them; and they shall be unto thee for the calling of the congregation, and for causing the camps to set forward. (Numbers 10:2)

According to the Talmudic sources, in Temple times the priests on Rosh Hashanah would position themselves so that the trumpet-blowers stood on either side, with the shofar in the middle since the shofar was the essential part of the Rosh Hashanah ritual. On all other occasions, the trumpet-blowers were in the middle, flanked by a shofar-blower on either side. In any event, the shofar and the trumpets complemented one another.

Rabbi Abraham Isaac Kook dew on the symbolism of the trumpets when considering the theological implications of the complex world that has resulted from the advances of modern science and technology, with all the heavy demands these have made on the human spirit.

The gains of this new way of manipulating nature are obvious. Our homes are illumined at the touch of a switch. We can travel easily from place to place so that the whole world has become one. Comforts and other benefits undreamed of by our ancestors are widely available. However, on the negative side, the danger looms of soul-destroying enslavement to the machine. As early as the nineteenth century, the cry of 'back to nature!' began to be heard – the claim that mankind can save its soul only by returning to the simple life.

The trouble is that, once having tasted the fruits of science and technology, most people have no desire to restore the old order even if such a thing were possible.

Judaism teaches that God created an incomplete world which it is the task of human beings to bring to greater perfection. The recognition that this task is God-given frees the human spirit so that humans refuse, in the language of tradition, to 'bow down to the work of their hands'.

The shofar, the instrument found in its natural form, represents the world of nature before man has begun to adapt nature to his needs. The silver trumpets, skilfully fashioned by human hands, represent human creative ability to refashion the world. For, after all, from the religious standpoint, all things come from God. As the Psalmist says (98:6): 'With trumpets and the sound of the shofar, give a joyful shout to the King, the Lord.'

> *Now the man Moses was very meek, above all the men that*
> *were on the face of the earth.*   (Numbers 12:3)

Moses, the greatest of men, is described as the meekest of men. This hardly accords with popular views about humility. For most people humility means that a man of little ability and few attainments should acknowledge to himself as well as to others what he is really like and not try to imagine himself to be superior. But how can a man who has done well in one field or another avoid feeling proud of himself? In our verse you have Moses, the great leader of his people out of bondage, the man head and shoulders above the most talented and most saintly of his brethren, and yet he is described as 'meek above all the men that were on the face of the earth'. How can this be? Many answers have been given. Here is noted the treatment of the subject in the writings of Rabbi Meir Simhah of Dvinsk in Latvia (1843–1926).

Rabbi Meir Simhah quotes a comment on our verse by his grandfather, Rabbi Hananiah Ha-Kohen.

The philosophers, says Rabbi Hananiah, have raised the general question regarding humility. How is it possible for a man of high worth and many talents and achievements to imagine himself to be inferior to those lacking in such qualities? If we recognize the worth of others, is it not merely a lack of perception to fail to recognize our own worth? Rabbi Meir Simhah writes that much has been written on the subject yet he rather likes his grandfather's observation on Moses. From this point of view Moses did know himself and was in no way guilty of self-delusion. How could Moses not have been aware that he alone had ascended the mountain to receive the Torah from God? But, by virtue of that very fact, Moses, in his humility, imagined that he was no longer a freely choosing human being. Having seen God 'face to face', all doubt had become impossible for him. Having seen the value and significance of the precepts, how could he possibly choose not to obey them? Thus Moses was humble in the sense that he believed he could no longer claim any credit or merit in being a good man. His experience had made him into an automaton, virtually obliged to do good. This is perhaps the meaning of 'all the men that were upon the face of the earth'. Moses felt himself to be inferior to men on earth who had not ascended to Heaven, as he had, and who were still capable of pursuing the good by their own free choice.

Faith had become impossible for Moses since faith involves acceptance on trust of that which one cannot actually comprehend. Moses had actually 'seen' God and for him there was never again any need to invoke faith. This is reminiscent of the Hasidic master who once remarked that, while there are tales of the prophet Elijah appearing to the saints, if he were offered a vision of Elijah he would refuse it, because such a confirmation of the truths he had hitherto held by faith, would serve to deprive him of man's most precious gift – his freedom of choice and his moral character.

38

Shelah

There is a remarkable interpretation of the command to fix *tzitzit* to the corners of the garment (Numbers 15:37–41) given by the famed Talmudist and religious thinker, Rabbi Meir Simhah of Dvinsk, whose commentary has been referred to previously. In many Jewish sources, Rabbi Meir Simhah notes, the universe is compared to a garment which God wears. A garment, in a sense, effectively conceals its wearer in that he is not seen as he really is underneath his clothes.

The glory of God fills the universe, but only those with eyes to see can gaze beyond appearances to perceive the divine energy which keeps all things in existence.

It is only as a result of God's concealment in the garment that is the universe that finite creatures can endure. Human beings, in the world of matter as well as of spirit, need the barrier provided by the material world if they are not to dissolve into nothingness in the face of the Infinite.

The universe is thus both a means of perceiving the divine power and glory and the means of concealing these in their fullness. Moreover, the material universe is in an unfinished state. This is intended by God so that humans can become partners with Him in bringing the world to ever greater perfection.

On the analogy of the garment, the world is like a precious robe the weaving of which has not been fully completed. According to Jewish law, the *tzitzit* have to be woven especially for the purpose of the *mitzvah*. They represent symbolically the completion by man of the weaving of God's garment.

In the same vein, Rabbi Meir Simhah gives his interpretation of circumcision. God has created superfluities in His universe, of which the foreskin is typical. The existence of these superfluities is part of the incomplete and imperfect universe it is the task of humans to make perfect and whole.

The covenant with Abraham represents the utter dedication of Abraham's seed, to strive to be servants of God by co-operating with Him in attending, as it were, to His unfinished business that He has left to man to finish. This thought Rabbi Meir Simhah finds in the Midrash. Here Turnus Rufus, Roman Governor of Palestine, asks Rabbi Akiba: 'If your God wants man to be circumcised why did He create the foreskin?' Rabbi Akiba replies that the removal of the foreskin is symbolic of the human effort God requires for the fulfilment of His purpose.

The precept of *tzitzit* has exercised the symbolists throughout the ages. Originally, as our passage states, there was to be a 'thread of blue' (*petil tekhelet*) in the *tzitzit*.This was later omitted since the method of dyeing the thread was unknown. It is, none the less, the custom of manufactures of the *tallit*, the shawl to which *tzitzit* are attached, to have woven into the fabric a blue strip as a reminder of the ancient practice. In a famous Midrashic comment, Rabbi Meir (second century) said that the *tekhelet* resembles in its colour the sea. The sea resembles the sky in its colour and the sky the Throne of Glory. Thus man is led to reflect on the colour of the thread and from there on the mighty seas and from there to the over-reaching sky. From there he is led to reflection on the divine glory which fills the universe and yet is beyond the universe.

The traditional method of inserting the *tzitzit* is also rich in symbolism. To mention one of these, four threads are inserted in each corner of the *tallit*. These are then doubled to form eight threads, four on each side of the corner. These eight threads are said to correspond to the eight days that elapsed from the Exodus from Egypt until the Israelites sang the song of deliverance at the sea (Exodus 15). The threads are tied into five knots and these correspond to the Five Books of Moses (the Pentateuch); the four corners into which the threads are inserted represent the need to be reminded of God and His law at every turn. Abraham Ibn Ezra, in his Commentary to the law of *tzitzit* understands the reminder on the analogy of the man who ties a knot in a garment (as we do nowadays in a handkerchief) to remind him of that which he does not want to forget.

In other words, frail human beings are incapable of awareness at all times of the eternal truths. They need constant reminders of the spiritual side of existence. All this is a key to the other precepts of the Torah. These, in addition to their supreme significance as divine commands, also have a symbolic sense in that they represent abstract truths in an available form.

39

Korah

In the nineteenth century there lived a Hasidic Rebbe who claimed that in a previous incarnation he lived in the time of Korah's rebellion against Moses. He further claimed to have memory of the ancient conflict. The Hasidim asked him whose side was he on, to which the Rebbe replied that he was neutral. But surely, the Hasidim protested, the Rebbe should have sided with Moses. Korah's arguments, said the Rebbe, were so persuasive that it was hard enough for me to remain neutral let alone to take the side of Moses.

We can sympathize with the Rebbe. Viewed superficially Korah was a democrat and an upholder of the rights of man. Korah vehemently objected to Moses' assumption of leadership and his claim to be superior to the people of God: 'All the congregation are holy, why do you raise yourself against them?' was Korah's passionate plea, awakening an echo in the souls of even the most devout reader of Scripture.

Today, when everyone is convinced of the value of democratic forms of government, we tend to see Korah as a champion of popular rule. Subconsciously, at least, we admire Korah's courage and see the point he appears to be making. The basic difference between the child's view of the Bible and that of the adult is that the child cannot sympathize with the villains of the Bible and cannot find fault with the Biblical heroes. The child tends to see things in clearly defined lines of black and white. Grey is largely unknown to him. The adult, on the other hand, knows from experience the complexities of human nature. He discovers, as he was meant to discover, that the heroes of the Bible, for all their greatness, were creatures of flesh and blood; in this lies their greatness. They had their faults, often serious faults. At the same time, he sees that the 'villains' of the Bible were not unredeemed through flashes of benevolence and good sense. The adult reads his Bible for it to throw light on human nature and seeks to understand why it is that in it some men and women are praised, for all their faults, and others denigrated, for all their virtues. The story of Korah demands such an approach. The question we must ask is, why does Scripture ultimately condemn Korah, placing him among the villains rather than among the heroes?

It is a great mistake to read the story of Korah to mean that Korah desired equality for all, while Moses favoured aristocracy and élitism. Moses also desired that all his followers should be great. When Eldad and Medad prophesied in the camp, Moses replied to Joshua's implication that this was an insult to him: 'Art thou jealous for my sake? Would that all the Lord's people were prophets that the Lord would put His spirit upon them' (Numbers 11:25–9).

Moses realized, however, that all the people were not prophets and the role of the leader chosen by God was to show them the truth seen by him to which all could aspire. Moses was the general who had reached the summit of the mountain and beckoned his troops to climb up nearer to the heights as God had shown him, even though they had not been chosen to go up all the way.

Translated into today's idiom. we might say that Moses desired equal spiritual equality for all, whereas Korah flattered themthat they already possessed all the greatness they needed, an idea that would eventually lead them to disaster. Korah was not a democrat. He was a demagogue, holding out to the people aims they could not possibly realize. It should not be forgotten that, in the whole narrative, Moses does not seek anything other for himself than to follow the word of God. He might even have preferred Korah to be the leader, but God had decided otherwise. In the Korah narrative we are not, in fact, really in the area in which men discuss political doctrines of equality. The whole narrative is meant to show that it is God, not Moses, who leads the people.

Something more on Korah was daringly said by another Hasidic master, Rabbi Mordecai Yosef of Izbica, grandfather of the Rebbe referred to at the beginning of this essay. According to Rabbi Mordecai Yosef, if Korah was no more than an ambitious rebel against authority, the Torah would have ignored him and certainly would not have devoted so much space to him. From the absolute standpoint, said Rabbi Mordecai Yosef, Korah was right that all God's people are holy; but this holy truth will be revealed only at the culmination of human history, the Messianic age. Korah's error was to anticipate the glorious future. Korah was guilty of realized eschatology.

This is the terrible but magnificent temptation of the religious idealist, to believe that all that needs to be achieved in human history will be achieved at once if only people will listen to him and see what he sees. Moses was right that there can be no anticipation of the Messianic age before God decrees that human history will find its fulfilment. When that age comes Korah will be seen to have been vindicated.

40

Hukkat

This is the law; when a man dieth in a tent.
(Numbers 19: 14)

The laws of corpse contamination and the purification rites recorded in this *sidra* are read before the festival of Passover. This practice is based on the need in Temple times for ritual purity when the people came to Jerusalem to offer the paschal lamb. The passage contains the laws of purification from the contamination resulting from contact with a dead body, the most severe form of contamination for the purification from which special rites had to be observed.

Nowadays, when the Temple service is no more and the purification rites no longer apply, our passage still serves to remind us that Judaism is a religion of life. One who has been face to face with death cannot directly appear before his Maker. Unlike the ancient Egyptian religion, whose priests were morbidly occupied with death and the fate of the soul in the nether world, the Hebrew religion aimed at the cultivation of life here on earth. The Hebrew priest was forbidden to come into contact with the dead. To this day at a funeral there is a special room, detached from the major room in which the coffin is laid, for the *Kohanim* so that they should not be in the same 'tent' as our *sidra* refers to it) as the corpse. A prominent student of comparative religion wrote that among no people is there a greater abhorrence of death and a greater love of life than among the Jews.

Yet the third-century teacher of Judaism, Resh Lakish, in a homily on our text, makes the striking comment that the Torah can become the permanent possession of the Jew only if he kills himself in its pursuit; that is, if he denies himself most of life's goods for the sake of the Torah. Is it not strange that a verse which expressly considers death to be a source of contamination should be given such an interpretation?

A deeper understanding of Resh Lakish's teaching enables us to see that there is no contradiction. He is giving expression to the paradox that without a denial of certain aspects of life there can be no embracing of a fuller life. The need for self-negation in the pursuit of an aim is true not only of the religious life but of everything for which it is worth striving Great art is impossible without the artist severely disciplining himself. Advances in knowledge and in science would be unthinkable without unqualified dedication of the scholar, the literary man and the scientist. Resh Lakish undoubtedly subscribes to the teaching behind the purification rites that our faith is centred on life, but he points out that life is not possible without denial.

This denial does not stem from a hatred of life, the masochistic pleasure of spurious martyrdom, but from a concentration on the deeper and more abiding things through a rejection of the more superficial and transitory aspects of human existence. It is the denial of a *Hillel* who, poor though he was, devoted a half of his earnings to the fee for admittance to the house of study, lying in the snow on the roof of the building in order to hear the lectures when he was refused admittance because of his inability to pay. It is the denial of a Rabbi Johanan who sold his fields and vineyards without thought of the morrow so that he could devote himself to the study of the Torah. It is the denial of countless Yeshivah students in pre-war Russia and Poland who spent their days in the toil of the Torah gladly giving up the glittering prizes in their love of the Torah. And it is the denial of the ordinary Jew who, in a thousand ways, makes sacrifices, and rejects many desirable things, in obedience to the will of his Father in Heaven.

There can be no true religion without a giving of the self in the service of the higher; there is no easy royal road to Judaism. It must be embraced the hard way and only then will it yield its delights. And we would not have it otherwise. There is something innate in man, a divine spark which refuses to take delight in things acquired too easily. The noble person wants above all to earn the rewards of spiritual life by labouring for them. The thrill of adventure, the element of risk, the obstacles in the path, these sharpen our enchantment when we reach our goal and make our pursuit of it more keen and more worthwhile. No self-respecting Jew would want a Judaism without tears, for a Judaism without tears would be a Judaism without bliss, without challenge and without joys.

THE RED HEIFER

The strange rites of the red heifer for purification, the theme of the beginning of our *sidra*, have been variously explained but have often been used to point to the mysterious element in religion, the element to which the saying in Ethics of the Fathers alludes:

> Where there is no wisdom, there is no fear of God; where there is no fear of God, there is no wisdom.

Few aspects of the religious life of Jews are more typical of the balanced sanity of historic Judaism than the equilibrium that is maintained between reason and religious emotion. The rationalistic trend in Jewish thought acted as a check to the vehemence of religious fervour, effectively preventing the religion from a ruining and unbridled fanaticism; and the movement towards ecstatic religion prevented the Jewish mind, nourished in intellectualism, from forming in itself a hard core of insensitivity to the strivings of the Jewish heart and soul.

The rites of the red heifer have often been interpreted to mean that reason has no place in Judaism just as reason is powerless when considering this puzzling rite; and yet to acknowledge this is itself an act of the unclouded reason and 'reasons' have been advanced to explain the rite. It is nonsense for a faith to give up reason since nonsense is nonsense and holy nonsense is still nonsense.

True, Judaism has had its anti-rationalists as well as teachers who, in the name of reason, tended to look askance on the whole mystical tradition in the Jewish religion. Yet, on the whole, the balance has been preserved in Jewish history between reason and sentiment. 'In Biblical times the ecstatic prophets existed side by side with the sober, precise priests who brought order into the Temple service. The Talmudic period produced the precise Halakhah, the legal side of Judaism, and Aggadah, the fruit of the imagination. In the Middle Ages, the Jewish philosophers gave expression in prose to the strivings of the Jewish spirit, the Kabbalists in wondrous and daring poetry. In more or less modern times, the Haskalah movement began the quest for a rational faith while the Hasidim said there was no such thing and gloried in religious ecstasy, often bordering on superstition. With exceptions, to be sure, but generally, the ideas behind the sayings in Ethics of the Fathers have been vindicated by Jewish teachers, that there can be no real wisdom without the fear of God and that the fear of God without wisdom is stultifying. Judaism is a religion of both, of the fear of God and of wisdom, the wisdom of the mind and the wisdom of the heart.

—41—

Balak

*Nevertheless, the Lord thy God would not hearken unto
Balaam; but the Lord thy God turned the curse into a
blessing unto thee, because the Lord thy God loved thee.*
(Deuteronomy 23:6)

This verse in Deuteronomy is part of Moses' summary of the events recorded in our *sidra* of how Balaam, the heathen prophet, sought to curse the people of Israel but God turned the curse into a blessing.

To the modern reader of the Bible the importance attached to Balaam's curse appears to be out of all proportion to its effects. Why was it necessary for God to change the curse into a blessing? What hidden power was there in the heathen prophet's malediction?

The student of psychology knows the strength and the effectiveness of constant suggestion. Fantastic though it seems at first glance, it is true that hundreds of sick people have been helped by the strenuous repetition of the affirmation: 'Every day and in every way I grow better and better.' Similarly, constant dwelling on a harmful idea has unhealthy effects on mind and body.

The influence of suggestion is doubly potent when applied in order to bring about mental failings. Tell a man often enough that he is a sinner and he will actually become one. This why the great Hasidic teachers, intensely aware though they were of the undoubted value of earnest heart-searching, nevertheless advised their followers against a morbid preoccupation with their sins. Balaam was the ancient prototype of the anti-Semitic propagandist, the ancestor of the calumniators of our times whose foul vituperations found their culmination in the destruction of

millions of innocent human beings. In addition to all the suffering
these creatures have brought upon Jews, they have at times scored
victories by winning over some of our people to subscribe in their
heart of hearts to their nefarious doctrines. 'There is no smoke
without fire,' say these folk to themselves, forgetting Hitler's
maxim that the bigger the lie the more readily will it be accepted,
and they begin to believe evil of their own people and to lose their
self-respect as members of that people.

God had to change Balaam's curse into a blessing. As a famous
sage and prophet, his pronouncements were accepted as expressions of unqualified truth. The implications of Balaam's denuncia-
tions would have acted as slow poison corroding the minds of the
Israelites and denuding them of the initiative required to enter
the promised land and become worthy of their eventual role of the
chosen people.

The lesson is clear. Jews must learn to think well of their people,
not in any narrow or chauvinistic spirit, but in a sincere attempt to
produce success by thinking it. Jews must never make the mistake
of imagining that the base lies spread about us are, even in some
small measure, really true. We remember those of the Greek
writers who informed the ignorant that deep in the Temple Jews
had the head of an ass which they worshipped in secret. In the
Middle Ages the majority of people believed in the magic power of
the Jew to poison the wells and that the ritual murder calumny
was based on fact. In the twentieth century many were duped by
The Protocols of the Elders of Zion.

All these are reminders that scurrilous and ridiculous lies have
been repeated about Jews without a single shred of truth in them,
and that it is our duty to ourselves to recognize them as such.
Criticize ourselves we must – self-criticism has always been a
Jewish virtue, one often overdone – but we must never imagine
ourselves to be depraved; that way is the path to national and
spiritual suicide. By remembering that we are the people which
gave to the world the monotheistic ideal as well as the ideals of justice and righteousness under God, we can gain inspiration to face
the future and we can repeat to our detractors the words
addressed to Balaam: 'Thou shalt not curse the people; for they are
blessed!'

Phinehas

Phinehas the son of Eleazar, the son of Aaron the priest, hath turned My wrath away from the children of Israel, in that he was very jealous for My sake among them ... Wherefore say: Behold, I give unto him My covenant of peace.   Numbers 25:11–12)

Phinehas, who slays the Israelite prince and the Midianite princess, is described as a man zealous for his God. He is the prototype of all those who cannot tolerate evil-doing and are prepared to resort even to extreme violence to achieve their ends.

Early on in the history of Judaism, on the other hand, attempts were made to treat the whole Phinehas episode as a once-and-for-all event, never to be repeated or emulated.

For instance, the Rabbis state that if Phinehas had asked Moses for an actual ruling, Moses would have told him that it was wrong to kill Zimri. It was only because Phinehas acted spontaneously in the face of a threat to the whole future of God's people, if they had succumbed to the blandishments of the Baal worshippers, that his act was lauded.

It is interesting to note that the name *kanai* given to Phinehas is also the term for fanatic. The line between zeal and fanaticism is very finely drawn; one can all too easily shade off into the other. There are, in the main, two basic differences between religious enthusiasm and fanaticism. The first is that the former is personal, refusing to interfere violently with the behaviour of others even when they are in the wrong. There is a Biblical injunction to rebuke wrongdoers, but this must be limited to verbal chastisement and, even then, must be done with tact and respect for human dignity. Actual punishment of wrongdoing is left to the courts, who are obliged to proceed by the due processes of law, otherwise vigilantism inevitably results in anarchy and is utterly self-defeating. Taking the law into one's own hands is lawlessness.

The second difference is that the true religious believer knows far better when not to display his zeal than when to display it. He reserves his enthusiasm for things that really matter. The fanatic tends to blur the distinction between the important and the comparatively trivial. Not only cannot he see the wood for the trees, but he imagines single trees to be a wood. A follower of the Kotzker Rebbe asked the master: 'Why do they call me a fanatic? I am simply a good Jew zealous for his religion.' The Rebbe replied: 'A fanatic is one who converts a minor issue into a major issue.'

In Hasidism enthusiasm is called *hitlahavut*, from *lahav*, 'a flame'. For the heart to be aflame for God, if this is authentic and not spurious, is no doubt commendable; but, like fire, it can be a destructive force unless it is controlled by the balanced critique of a sober mind.

PHINEHAS, THE SON OF ELEAZAR, THE SON OF AARON THE PRIEST

Why was it necessary, ask the Rabbis, to give the genealogy of Phinehas? It was precisely because his act was dubious and because, on his mother's side, he was descended from Putiel, identified with a former idolatrous priest, that he might have been suspected of killing the prince out of resentment that he was not himself of noble descent. Scripture tells us that, on his father's side, he was a true aristocrat.

Jews have always placed good family high on the list of qualifications for the suitors of their sons and daughters. 'A man should sell all he possesses in order to marry the daughter of a scholar,' is a typical Rabbinic saying. Many are the Jewish stories of matchmakers waxing eloquent over a young man or woman's distinguished ancestry.

Nowadays, the idea of *yihus* has fallen into disfavour and is considered to be politically incorrect. Our tendency is to see it as slightly ridiculous that a man or woman's worth be assessed by what his or her parents or grandparents were, rather than by what they themselves are. There is much point in the anecdote about the famous rabbi, the son of a simple tailor, who, when taunted by his rabbinic colleagues, descended from long lines of rabbis, replied:

'My sainted father, of blessed memory, used to say, it is better to have a suit made specially for your boy than to alter his father's old clothes to fit him.'

And yet the ancient Rabbis, who attached so much importance to good family, were not eugenic faddists, and it would a short-sighted policy that dismisses entirely the *yihus* idea as of no consequence. For one thing, the traditional Jewish aristocracy was one of learning and character and was thus open to any good and able man.

It is true that, at first, there existed a considerable degree of tension between the older aristocrats, the priests, and the new upper class of Torah scholars, but, to the advantage of Jewish life, it was the latter who won the day. A tremendous impetus to Jewish learning was one of the fruits of this victory. Pride of family can be overdone, but it can still serve as a spur to good and gracious Jewish living.

—43—

Mattot

Then ye shall be clear before the Lord, and before Israel.
(Numbers 32:22)

The tribe of Reuben and Gad found the land on the other side of the Jordan desirable and wished to possess this rich grazing land for their numerous flocks. When Moses reminds them that it was their duty to fight together with their brethren for the land on the other side of the Jordan, they declare their intention of doing so. Moses approves of their right decision, saying to them that by taking the correct course they will be 'clear before the Lord, *and before Israel'*. The Rabbis derive from this verse a great principle of conduct. It is necessary for people so to live that their conduct is endorsed by other human beings as well as by God. This principle is also found in the verse: 'so shalt thou find favour and good understanding in the sight of God and man' (Proverbs 3:4). Thus a man's conduct must never awaken suspicion that he is doing wrong even if his own conscience is clear.

This principle finds its expression in a number of instances. If charity collectors have a number of small coins which they cannot carry around with them and so wish to change these for a lesser number of coins of a larger denomination, they should not change the coins without others participating in the change, otherwise they might be suspected of appropriating some of the charity money. For the same reason there should always be two charity collectors not one. Two collectors can check each other's honesty. In Temple times, we are told, the families engaged in the preparation of the incense would not allow their womenfolk to use perfume so that no one should say that they were making profane use of the sacred materials. If a judge senses that one of the contestants before him tends to suspect him of favouritism, he must state clearly that his decision is based on sound legal precedent and that bias has not been allowed to sway his opinion.

On the face of it there is something offensive in this idea that we must not only satisfy God but our fellows as well. If we are clear in God's eyes, why should we be obliged to be clear in the eyes of men? Are we not taught by our religion to be true to our principles even if others condemn them? Can the man of independence tolerate having to look constantly over his shoulder to see what other people think of him? Can it be true that the good Jew has to think of what the neighbours will say?

A very clear distinction has to be made between two kinds of apparent wrongdoing. Jewish teaching is that I must not perform an act I know to be innocent and harmless if others think that it is wrong *where the standards they apply are accepted by them and by me as true Jewish standards.* But it is quite different where I disagree with them about the very standards they apply. When Abraham, for instance, defied idolatry to stand on one side with all the world on the other, it was an instance of a believer in the one God remaining faithful to Him no matter how many had different standards based on false gods and base conduct. No matter how many prostrate themselves to strange gods, the theist will never give way to their contemptible opinions.

Our text reminds us that we must try to be above suspicion of wrongdoing, for such suspicion may lead to a complete lowering of standards. Yet when all is said and done, we should not be so circumspect as to surrender entirely our own point of view. If we believe, after carefully weighing up the consequences, that our path is right, we should persist in it even if it happens to be unpopular. This is what counts, and then and only then can we hope to find favour and good understanding in the eyes of our fellows.

—44—

Masse

Here are the stages of the children of Israel. (Numbers 33:1)

God understandeth the way thereof, and he knoweth the place thereof. (Job 28:23)

The account, with which our *sidra* opens, of the stages reached by the ancient Israelites in their forty years of wandering through the wilderness, has always been considered to be the forerunner of the movements and journeys from place to place by Jews throughout their history. Rabbi Hiyya, the great second-century Babylonian teacher, applied the verse from the book of Job to the Jewish people. God understands the way of life of His people, said Rabbi Hiyya, and knew how impossible this would be if they were to be permanently under the harsh Roman occupation of the Land of Israel, so he exiled them to Babylonia, where they were to find a greater measure of religious freedom and toler-ance. Roman Palestine in Rabbi Hiyya's day was anything but favourable to the cultivation of Jewish ideals. Discriminatory laws and heavy taxation made the political situation, if not entirely precarious – there were good periods after all – yet uncertain to say the least.

In Babylon, on the other hand, Jews were accorded equal rights with the other citizens of the great Persian Empire. Jews were allowed a degree of autonomy and the freedom to live their own lives. Jews were even allowed to have their own ethnic-religious organizations, with the Exilarch as virtually a Jewish king, with his own court and soldiers. Here in Babylonia Jews could live freely as Jews, and it was in Babylon that Jews reciprocated Persian bene-volence. The younger contemporary of Rabbi Hiyya, Mar Samuel, laid down the rule that the law of the kingdom is as binding upon Jews as Jewish law.

This has always been the experience of the Jews in their long and distinctive history. Wherever Jews were treated as equals, where they were received in friendship, they embraced the land which made them welcome. The Sassanian rulers were benevolently disposed toward, the Jews on account of the expertise of the latter in commerce. The Babylonian Talmud, produced in this period, is, of course, the great monument to Rabbinic learning. Observing the Babylonian attitude towards the Jews, Rabbi Hiyya did well to remark that because God knows the nature of His people He exiled them to Babylon.

History repeats itself. Jews settled in Alexandria in Egypt before Rabbi Hiyya's day and the specific type of Greek culture made its way into Jewish life. The same thing happened when Jews settled in Spain, Italy, France, Russia and Poland. Each 'stage' of Jewish wandering produced its own particular type of Jewishness, so to speak. The sorry tale of the Russian persecution of the Jews and the terrible events in Nazi Germany are all too well known; and in the twentieth century, the Jews wandered again, but this time not in exile, but to the homeland of Eretz Israel.

The journeys of the children of Israel recounted in our *sidra* were not all in sadness or with tragic events. There were, no doubt, many of these, but there were glorious events as well, the most elevated being the revelation at Sinai. The same applies to the other wanderings of the Jews through the various lands. We should reject what the historian Salo Baron calls the lachrymose view of Jewish history. As, in the words of Rabbi Hiyya, God understood the nature of His people, He led them not only through vales of tears but also through spacious uplands in which they could sing joyfully to the God of their fathers.

All this sounds more than a little hollow after the Holocaust. It is futile and even grossly impious to inquire why God should have desired His people to suffer the searing agony of the most terrible event in all their wandering. When we continue to read our *sidra* and its tale of wanderings from place to place, it is not a theodicy of wandering that we can extract. Such terrible questions as haunt us can only be left to God Himself. What the narrative of the journeys can do for us is to remind us that, somehow, the Jewish people can never find permanent security of place, and yet the faithful Jews, journeying under God, can and have found a measure of permanence in every land in which they find themselves, for, ultimately, their journey is towards eternity. For the God they worship is the eternal God and every place is filled with His glory. There is an old Hasidic saying which runs as follows: 'He whose place is nowhere has a place everywhere.'

PART SIX
DEUTERONOMY/*DEVARIM*

45

Devarim

These are the words which Moses spoke to all Israel.
(Deuteronomy 1:1)

In a typical Midrashic comment on this verse, the Hebrew for 'the words', *ha-devarim*, is read as if it were *ha-devorim*, 'the bees' (the consonants of both words are the same). Thus the verse is made to read: 'These are the *bees* which Moses spoke to all Israel.' According to this homily, Moses' words to all Israel were 'bees', that is, they were bee-like in nature. A number of interpretations are given for this strange simile.

The first is that the words of the righteous and the prophets can be compared with a swarm of bees as people throng to follow their teachings which guide Jews throughout the world. Perhaps the meaning here is that though each good man and prophet is an individual, his specific insights are of value to the whole group.

Another interpretation is that bees produce honey but they can also sting. Moses' words of stinging rebuke were also honeyed words, sweet in their effect. It is a common failure to see religious truth in sugary terms. The Torah, however, has its stern aspects, punishing wrongdoers who make life sour. Without its sting the bee would not exist as a bee and we would not have the benefit of its honey. Some tend to see the Torah as an unchallenging piece of sentimentalism, but the truly devout would not wish to have a religion without its aches and pains, without the difficulties which alone afford protests against evil. The Midrash elaborates still further, that for the unworthy the Torah itself is perilously stinging, which may mean that there are those for whom their religion is all threats of punishment and harshness.

Still another interpretation is, just as everything the bee gathers it gathers for its owner, so, too, whatever merits and good deeds Israel accumulates it accumulates for the glory of its Father in Heaven. On this view the performance of the precepts of the Torah is not for the purpose of self-glorification but for the glory of God.

> *Get you, from each one of your tribes, wise men, and understanding and full of knowledge, and make them heads over you...So I took the heads of your tribes, wise men and full of knowledge, and made them heads over you...*   (Deuteronomy 1: 13–15)

Moses has to delegate his authority so he asks the people to choose men who would serve as judges in his stead. The qualifications Moses requires of the leaders and judges are that they should be wise men *(hakhamim)*, men of understanding *(nevonim)* and men full of knowledge *(yeduim)*; but in the later verse it refers only to *hakhamim* and *yeduim*, upon which the Rabbis comment that Moses was unable to find anyone with all three qualifications. There were *hakhamim* and *yeduim* but no *nevonim*. Obviously, no one could serve as a judge unless he had knowledge of the law and was wise enough to apply it; but the quality of understanding, the ability to apply analogical reason was rare, and in its absence Moses had to make do with men with the other two qualifications.

In the Jewish mystical tradition, these verses are applied not only to judges but to mystical adepts. The mystic had to be wise in the sense of mystical awareness and he had to have knowledge of the intricacies and complexities of the Kabbalah, the great theosophical system. It was a bonus if, at the same time, he had powers of discernment. Yet for some of the Hasidic leaders, 'men of understanding' meant those who engaged in philosophical interpretation of the Torah. From this point of view, Moses did not find *nevonim* because the absence of rational inquiry, far from being a fault in religion, was a positive benefit. In the history of Judaism there is often tension between the mystical and the rationalistic approaches. Yet in some great teachers the two were combined. Even the supreme rationalist among the medieval philosophers, Maimonides, had a mystical turn to his thought, as can be seen by one who studies Maimonides' philosophical work, *The Guide to the Perplexed*.

The lesson of all this for those who study the Torah is that the student should have keen comprehension but not be 'too clever by half'. He should master the subject and know it thoroughly, he should have more than a superficial knowledge of the facts of his studies, and have powers of discernment. In the middle ages they used to call a student who had vast stores of knowledge but without really understanding them, 'a donkey carrying books'.

> *And I charged your judges at that time, saying: 'Hear the causes between your brethren, and judge righteously between a man and his brother, and the stranger that is with him'.*   (Deuteronomy 1:16)

The Rabbis apply the words 'between your brethren' to mean that a judge must not listen to the claims of one of the men brought before him unless both men are present. He must hear the claims 'between' his brethren. Not only is the judge debarred from taking sides but he must not even appear to be taking sides, as he would be if he were to hear each one out in the absence of the other. He must listen to both sides. In the moralistic literature, this is taken as a lesson to everyone to weigh up carefully both sides of the question when making a decision.

> *How can I myself alone bear your cumbrance, and your burden, and your strife?*   (Deuteronomy 1:12)

The Hebrew word for 'How', *ekhah*, is the opening word of the book of Lamentations. It has been arranged that this *sidra* is always read on the Sabbath before the fast of the Ninth of Av, when Jews mourn for the destruction of the Temples and other calamities which took place at this time. The 'How' of Moses thus parallels the 'How' of Lamentations. 'How' is more an exclamation than a question. 'How can such a thing have happened?' is the bitter cry wrung from a heart contemplating the horrors of the past.

The advisability of such dwelling on the past is often questioned. Can our mourning bring the dead back to life or undo the tragedy? Is it not more sound psychologically to think of the future and its hopes instead of morbidly concentrating on the past and its disasters? Nowadays, with the establishment of the State of Israel, questions of this kind have assumed special significance.

Three considerations should not be overlooked. First, we do not mourn so much for the dead as for those left behind. Maimonides records, in his great Code, that one who refuses to mourn the death of a near relative is cruel. He is cruel because he demonstrates that his heart is insensitive to his loss. Judaism does believe that the soul is immortal and yet Jewish tradition prescribes detailed rituals of grief and mourning when a near relative dies. Judaism does not encourage stoical indifference to pain. It is the callous person who remains unmoved and unaffected when death takes its toll of someone near and dear to him.

Second, to think on the failures of the past provides the most powerful spur for redressing evils and the laying of more sure foundations for the building of the future.

Third, and most important of all, the Jew mourns not alone for the physical sufferings of his people, grievous though these have been, but for the exile of the Shekhinah – for the Divine Presence still well-nigh excluded from a world torn and divided by suspicion, fear, prejudice and hatred between man and man, and nation and nation. The illustration given by the old-time Maggidim, naïve though it is, is germane to the issue. A father set aside each week a portion of his hard-earned wages as savings for the education of his only child. He placed the money he had saved in a beautifully wrought money-bag. One day the child took the bag out of the drawer and, carelessly playing with it, allowed it to fall into the fire. The child weeps at the loss of the trinket, but the father weeps for the banknotes it contained, which could have made such a contribution to the child's future. We bewail the loss of the Temple burnt in fire, but God, as it were, weeps for all that the Temple stood for, for the holiness and goodness and peace banished largely from earth when the holy Temple was destroyed. Seen in this way, mourning over the darkness itself is a cause of hope and celebration in the future, which is why the three weeks of mourning culminating in the Ninth of Av are followed by seven weeks of consolation.

46

Vaethanan

And I besought the Lord at that time. (Deuteronomy 3:23)

Moses tells the people how he offered supplication that God should allow him to enter the Promised Land. He prayed *at that time*. It is interesting to note that, like the prayer of Moses, all the prayers in the Bible are those of individuals offered as the time arose, that is, when the opportunity presented itself. Congregational prayers at fixed times came later in Judaism but now form the essential pattern of Jewish worship in the synagogue; and even when an individual prays on his own he is still expected to adopt the standard forms. For all that, the Jewish masters of prayer advise, when an individual has specific needs he should ask God to answer his prayer for them. The fixed forms are necessary if Jewish worship is not to disintegrate through each individual inventing his or her own form and vocabulary. Yet the advice about individual prayer introduces spontaneity and prevents prayer from becoming too lifeless and irrelevant to personal needs.

> *But ye that did cleave unto the Lord your God are alive every one of you this day.* (Deuteronomy 4:4)

In the context this verse means that, unlike the worshippers of Baal Peor, mentioned in the previous verses, you, the people who worship only the true God, were not destroyed but are still alive this day. Thus the Hebrew word for 'who did cleave', the word *hadevekim*, means those who attached themselves to God and not to the false god of Baal Peor. For the Rabbis of the Midrash, however, 'to cleave' denotes a much stronger sense of attachment and they ask, how can finite human beings become firmly fixed to God? And they reply that while real attachment to God is impossible yet human beings can become intimately devoted to God's Torah and this devotion is intended by attachment to God since the Torah is the word of God.

Among the Jewish mystics, the idea was developed of *devekut*, derived from the word in our verse *hadevekim*. For the mystics *devekut* is a state of mind in which God is always present. Maimonides describes this state of mind on the analogy of a love-sick man who cannot get his beloved out of his mind, thinking of her all the time. In most versions of Hasidism, *devekut* is essential to the religious life, though the more realistic of the Hasidic masters taught that *devekut* at all times is possible only for the very greatest of saints and, even for them, there is an ebb and flow of the divine presence in the heart and mind. For lesser men, they taught, human beings should endeavour to come as close as possible to God when they offer their prayers. The *Mitnaggedim*, the traditionalist opponents of the Hasidim, did not believe that real *devekut* was possible in this world. Only when the soul has flown the body will it be able to be actually attached to God in some way beyond our understanding. Hasidim have special melodies without words in which the soul's yearning for God are given expression. Such a melody is known as a *devekut niggun*, an attachment or devotional melody.

THE DECALOGUE

The Ten Commandments or the Decalogue (a better word since they are referred to as the Ten Words, not Ten Commandments) are found in two versions: one in our *sidra* (Deuteronomy 5:6–19), which Moses repeats, and the other, in which is described the original giving of the Decalogue (Exodus 20:1–14). Although the wording is slightly different in the two versions (Ibn Ezra attributes the difference to the fact that Moses is reporting the giving of the commandments and reported speech differs from direct speech), in both the actual injunctions are the same, ten in number and presented in the same order:

1. I am the Lord thy God.

2. To have no other gods.
3. Not to bear God's name in vain.
4. Keep the Sabbath.
5. Honour father and mother.
6. Do not murder.
7. Do not commit adultery.
8. Do not steal.
9. Do not bear false witness.
10. Do not covet.

Whole books have been written on the Decalogue and sermons, Jewish and non-Jewish, without number have been delivered on the theme. Here each 'commandment' is treated in a homiletical fashion in an attempt to show the meaning and elaboration of each according to the Jewish tradition and how each can be applied in contemporary Jewish life.

1. *'I am the Lord thy God'*

This not a *command* (another reason for preferring the word Decalogue) but rather a preamble to the whole, the meaning being: 'I am the Lord your God who brought you out of Egypt and therefore I command you as follows.' Some, like Maimonides, do understand this as a command, but not a command to believe that God exists. It would be absurd for God to command us to believe that He exists since if we already believe, there is no point to the command and if we do not believe there is no one to command. If it is a command it must mean a command to have proper trust in the God who led us out of Egypt.

2) *'Thou shalt have no other gods before Me. Thou shalt not make unto thee a graven image, even any manner of likeness, of anything that is in heaven above, or that is in the earth beneath, or that is in the water beneath the earth'*

Two commands are included here, though they are counted as one. No other than God is to be worshipped and no graven images of the gods are to be fashioned. According to Jewish law, no benefit whatsoever may be had from an idol or from something offered in worship to an idol. In Talmudic times, the Rabbis sternly forbade anything that would seem to give substance to idols precisely because educated Romans in the first and second centuries in

Palestine were idolaters, at least on the surface level. The Mishnah records that Rabban Gamaliel used to bathe in a bath-house in which there was a statue of Aphrodite, defending his practice on the grounds that the statue was not an object of worship but simply ornamental. 'People do not say: "Let us build a bath-house for Aphrodite" but "Let us make an Aphrodite for our bath-house."' These laws were applied in Christian lands to the crucifix and similar Christian symbols. It was all part of the battle against idolatrous worship which had its origin in our verse and in many other Biblical verses.

The Hasidic master, Rabbi Mordecai Yosef of Izbica, has a novel and daring interpretation of 'in the heaven above and on the earth beneath' in our passage. According to his understanding, that which is in the heaven above refers to the Sabbath, the sacred day which is determined from Heaven; and on the earth beneath refers also to the most sacred object on earth, the Temple. Thus the meaning is given that, for all his reverence for the Sabbath and the Temple, the Jew must see these not as things to be worshipped but as a means to the worship of God. Even the Torah is a means to come to God and is never to be itself an object of worship. The sixteenth-century Italian Rabbi, Joseph de Trani, went so far as to forbid Jews to bow to the Torah. Most Jews today do bow to the Torah and to the Ark in the synagogue, but that is not as an act of worship but purely as a token of respect, much as we bow to a man we wish to honour.

3. *Not to take God's name in vain*

In the context, this refers to taking a vain oath in the court, to swear falsely in a court of law in order to substantiate one's claim. This was developed, however, to mean that one should not be so familiar with the divine as to invoke God's name unnecessarily, which is why some pious Jews today will say 'Hashem' (the 'Name') instead of using 'God' even in a sacred context, where the substitution is unwarranted. Certainly the spelling G-d, currently found in English writings, is precious and a species of one-upmanship not required by Jewish law.

A further idea that has been read into the third commandment is not to invoke God's name for one's own selfish purposes, to pretend that we are obeying God when we are, in fact, pursuing our own aims and ambitions. In a Midrashic comment, the verse is applied to a sinful person wearing *tefillin* as a cloak to his misdeeds. Such a person bears God's name in the *tefillin* in vain. This is a protest against the nefarious deeds all too often performed by religious people claiming to be obeying God.

4. *'Keep the Sabbath'*

The command to refrain from work on the Sabbath does not mean that just as God created His work of creation on the seventh day so, too, we must cease from our normal activities on the Sabbath. It is not implied that keeping the Sabbath involves *Imitatio Dei*. From the two versions of the Decalogue three reasons emerge for the command to keep the Sabbath holy: it is a reminder of God the Creator; it is a reminder of the Exodus; and it is to enable slaves to have a day of rest.

5. *'Honour thy father and thy mother'*

In the Jerusalem Talmud the fifth commandment is seen as a perfectly natural obligation to pay our debt to those who brought us into the world. There are three partners in the creation of human beings, the father, the mother and the Almighty, so that by honouring and paying respect to our human parents we are honouring and paying respect to God as well as to them. Nevertheless, according to Jewish law, if parents wish to forgo the honour due to them, their son and daughter are released from the obligation.

In the Jewish tradition the fifth commandment is extended to older siblings, grandparents, parents-in-law and step-parents. It also embraces teachers. A typical Rabbinic saying is that a man has a greater obligation to honour his teacher than to honour his father since his father brought him into this world while the teacher who taught him the Torah brings him into the World to Come, to eternal bliss in the Hereafter.

The great moral question that arises in connection with the fifth commandment is the extent to which children must go in honouring their parents. The Codes discuss this question and generally tend to place limits on parental demands where these are in conflict with the strong personal needs of the children. For instance, the accepted ruling is that a son is not obliged to give up a woman whom he wishes to marry because his father disapproves of the match. In the early days of the Hasidic movement, when strong parental disapproval was voiced against the young men journeying to the Hasidic masters and embracing the new pattern of life, the masters retorted that the fifth commandment does not demand that a person should sacrifice his spiritual needs in favour of his father's opinions. There are numerous instances in the Talmud and in the later Rabbinic literature of fathers and sons in strong disagreement in matters of law and commentary on the Torah.

6. 'Thou shalt not kill'

Actually, as the medieval commentator, Rabbi Samuel ben Meir, pointed out, the Hebrew *lo tirtzah* should be translated as 'Thou shalt not murder', so that the sixth commandment does not cover every act of killing, in self-defence, for example. Nor does it cover abortion since a foetus is not considered to be a full person in Jewish law. Abortion is, of course, a severe sin and is normally strictly forbidden but there are circumstances – where, for example, the mother's life is in danger through childbirth – in which an abortion is allowed, as it would not be if foeticide were treated as homicide. Naturally these matters are left to the Jewish lawyers. What does emerge from the sixth commandment and from many other passages in the Bible is that Jews should have, and have had, the strongest aversion to the taking of human life. Also the Jewish teachers include other lesser offences under the heading of the sixth commandment, which, though not actually murder, share, to some extent, the severity of a murder. For instance, the Talmud states that to put a man to shame in public is *as if* the man's blood had been shed.

7. 'Thou shalt not commit adultery'

In the context, adultery means sexual relations with a married woman by a man other than her husband. In ancient times a man could have more than one wife so that his marriage bond did not preclude him from having sex with a woman other than his wife. Nowadays, polygamy is banned under Jewish law and a husband is expected to be as faithful to his wife as his wife is to him. In any event, while not covered by the seventh commandment, sex outside marriage is treated as fornication and is forbidden. Men and women do frequently live together as man and wife even though they are not technically married, and Nahmanides in medieval Spain permitted concubinage. However, Jews are expected to uphold the high standards of sexual morality, and the marriage of one man to one woman, each forsaking all others, is the ideal of Jewish marriage.

On the principle of *as if*, mentioned earlier, the Talmudic Rabbis say that to take away a man's livelihood by causing him to lose his job or by ruining his business is *as if* he had taken the man's life. The seventh commandment is also extended by the Rabbis to undue familiarity with another man's wife: flirting with her, for example, or sexual arousal by hugging and kissing.

8. *'Thou shalt not steal'*

According to the Rabbis the eighth commandment covers only the capital offence of kidnapping. Thus the verse means: 'Thou shalt not steal a person.' Of course, there are other verses in the Bible which forbid all manner of theft and robbery. Plagiarism is forbidden since to steal another man's ideas is at least as much an act of theft as to steal his property.

9. *'Thou shalt not bear false witness against thy neighbour'*

In the context this refers to a man giving false testimony in a court of law. But, in subsequent Jewish teaching, it is made to refer also to judging others unfairly, as when the Rabbis say: 'Judge your neighbour in the scale of merit', i.e., find excuses for him when in doubt as to his actions. Another Rabbinic saying is: 'Judge not another until you have reached his place', i.e., do not condemn another until you have had the same kind of temptation and therefore appreciate how hard it was for him. Nevertheless, the contemporary aversion to being judgemental, if followed, would deprive us of the right to have strong opinions in matters of morals and religion. We have a right, for example, to criticize those in power over us, provided the criticism is fair and balanced.

10. *'Thou shalt not covet'*

Unlike the other commandments, this seems to control thoughts. The difficulty then arises, while we can, if we try, control our actions – we can stop at actually stealing even if we are inwardly inclined to do so – how can we help feeling covetous? Ibn Ezra's famous reply is well known. A peasant may dream of marrying a princess but, since he knows that, in reality, this will never happen, he does not deep down have a real desire to marry her, any more than a man has the slightest desire to marry his mother. According to Ibn Ezra, each person's destiny is laid down by divine Providence and it is as little possible for him to obtain that which God has determined for someone else as it is for the peasant to marry the princess. By this interpretation the tenth commandment is for a man to cultivate his trust in the divine apportioning of things, so that he becomes the kind of person who automatically refrains without effort from desiring the property of another or lusting after his wife.

In the Rabbinic tradition, however, the tenth commandment is a demand not to take any *action* that might result from coveting, i.e., not to plot and scheme so as eventually to gain control legally over another man's wife or his property. As this is generally developed by the less severe moralists, the matter is as follows. If I see that my friend is married to a desirable woman, I am not forbidden by the tenth commandment to say to myself: I would like to marry a woman like that man's wife. What I am forbidden to do is to say to myself: I must have that woman even though she is married to him. I hope and dream that he will die or that they will be divorced. Such thoughts can easily lead to acts of mischief which, while strictly within the law, may eventually bring about a rift in the marriage. Or, better, if my friend has, say, a Rolls-Royce, I am allowed to say to myself: I, too, would like to have a Rolls-Royce. What I must not say to myself is: I must get my hands on *that* Rolls-Royce and I must try to persuade him to sell it to me even though I am prepared to pay whatever he asks for it. Such thoughts will inevitably tempt me to illegal actions that bring about the desired consequences. Many Jews, nevertheless, have preferred to understand the tenth commandment as Ibn Ezra understands it, that it is a command to cultivate a serene attitude of trust in the belief that each person's lot in life is not under his control but under God's.

For all the importance of the Decalogue in Jewish life, a tendency is to be observed not to give it too much prominence in Jewish worship. In Temple times the priests used to recite before they began the service of the day, the Shema and the Decalogue. However, the attempt to have the Decalogue recited as part of the liturgy of the synagogue was defeated. The reason was, in all probability, that Christians should not claim that Jews, too, as they do, attach significance only to the Decalogue, not to the rest of the Torah. For this reason Maimonides was opposed to people standing when the Decalogue is read as part of the reading of our *sidra* in the synagogue. Nowadays it is the universal custom, nevertheless, to stand when the Decalogue is read in the synagogue. There is point in giving special honour to the Decalogue and no one is going to say that this implies that the rest of the Torah is unimportant, since the standing takes place during the reading of the *sidra* and hence as part of the whole Torah.

THE SHEMA

> *Hear, O Israel: The Lord our God, the Lord is One. And thou shalt love the Lord thy God with all thy heart, and with all thy soul, and with all thy might. And these words, which I command thee this day, shall be upon thy heart; and thou shalt teach them diligently unto thy children, and shall talk of them when thou sittest in thy house, and when thou walkest by the way, and when thou liest down, and when thou risest up. And thou shalt bind them for a sign upon thy hand, and they shall be for frontlets between thine eyes. And thou shalt write them upon the doorposts of thy house, and upon thy gates.* (Deuteronomy 6:4–9)

This passage in our *sidra*, known as the Shema ('Hear'), after its opening word, contains, and has been understood in the Jewish tradition to contain, the basic ideas of the Jewish religion. Like the Decalogue, the Shema has been the subject of hundreds of works and sermons throughout the ages. Short of trying to compile yet another book on the Shema, what I want to do here is to survey in a homiletical style some of the meaning and implications of a number of keywords.

First, consider the expression: 'Hear, O Israel'. In the context, the 'Israel' referred to is the people of Israel whom Moses was addressing. But, when Jews recite the Shema daily, to whom are they saying: 'Hear, O Israel'? One answer in the tradition is that they are addressing fellow-worshippers, calling on one another to hearken to the truth as the Seraphim call one to the other to proclaim 'Holy, holy, holy' (Isaiah 6:3). In a Midrashic interpretation, Jews are calling to the patriarch, Jacob, who was called Israel by God. They are saying: Hear, O Jacob/Israel, the Lord is our God as he was yours. We have kept and still keep the charge you gave to your descendants to be faithful to the covenant. In the mystical tradition, the thought is found that Jews are calling to their higher nature called Israel. They are calling upon their deeper selves to listen to the truth, the inner self which can hear even when outwardly they tend to forget.

The word *ehad*, 'one', in the context probably means alone, i.e., the verse is saying: 'The Lord alone is our God. There is no other.' However, in the history of Jewish interpretation the word *ehad* has received a number of different and ever deeper meanings. Thus the medieval Jewish philosophers translate *ehad* as 'unique'. According to the philosophers, the Shema is stating not only that there are no other gods but rather that since God is God there cannot be any other gods. God's essential nature is utterly beyond our comprehension but is so beyond anything humans understand by 'the gods'. Monotheism does not mean that, as a matter of fact, there is only one God, our God, though there might conceivably have been more than one. Monotheism means rather that the Source of all being is a unique Being with whom nothing can be compared. This is what the philosophers were claiming when, like Maimonides, they said that God as He is Himself can be known only through His attributes.

Among some of the Jewish mystics, especially the Habad thinkers, the word *ehad* denotes not only that God is one and unique, but that He is the only one to enjoy ultimate existence. Before God's essential Being the world and all that is in it is dissolved, as it were, so that, from the point of view of ultimate reality no creatures exist at all. This belief is often called 'pantheism' but a more helpful term is 'panentheism', 'all is in God', in the sense that the universe is in God but He is beyond the universe. This is a very difficult notion to fathom but so are all ideas about God's relation to the universe. The whole point of mentioning these various speculations is as a reminder of how impossible it is for humans to speak at all of God's essential nature. For the devout, it is sufficient and wholesome to leave speculation aside and recite the Shema as a simple affirmation that God *is*. That is all our religion expects us to do and is, in fact, the most sublime way of approaching the great mystery.

The Shema continues in the second verse: 'And thou shalt love the Lord thy God with all thy heart, and with all thy soul, and with all thy might.'

It should first be noted that, for the ancients, the 'heart' denotes all the inner being of man and the meaning is not so much the seat of the emotions as the intellect, the mind. Thus 'with all thy heart'

really means 'with all your mind'. The word 'soul' in the verse really refers to what we call the 'self'. Thus a translation more in keeping with current English usage would be 'with your whole self'. In
one Talmudic understanding, this means even if God takes your
whole self away you should love him, i.e., the Jew, in the rare
instances when this becomes necessary, must be ready to give up
his very life for the sake of God. Thus our verse became a key text
for the idea of martyrdom. This is hardly ever demanded in the
contemporary world. Instead we should be ready to make sacrifices in trying to live as a Jew. Adapting Bernard Shaw's saying:
Any fool can die for his religion but it takes a wise man to live for
his religion. When the great Jewish thinker, Mordecai
Kaplan,reached the age of ninety, after a lifetime of reflection on
Judaism, he said that only now had he come to appreciate that this
verse of the Shema means that you have to love God intellectually
('with all thy heart'), emotionally ('with all thy soul') and practically ('with all thy might').

THE LOVE OF GOD

Judaism, its critics persist in telling us, is a religion based on fear.
Wellhausen, for instance, long ago had this to say in a chapter on
'Jewish Piety':

> The motive of morals by which they become religious is the fear of God,
> God is a severe master. He rules vassals whom he calls from the dust,
> and again changes into dust.

How was it possible for Wellhausen, great Biblical scholar
though he was, to overlook the devout outburst of the Psalmist: 'As
the hart panteth after the water brooks, so panteth my soul after
thee, O God.' He must surely also have been aware of the book of
Deuteronomy, a book full of God's love for Israel and Israel's love
for God. Those who speak of Judaism as a religion of fear overlook
entirely our verse in the Shema: 'And thou shalt love the Lord thy
God, with all thy heart, and with all thy soul, and with all thy
might.' Tillich quotes this verse as the supreme statement of ultimate concern in religion.

Yes, the love of God is an essential part of the Jewish faith and
yet it is futile to imagine that this love is easy to attain. It is easy

enough to love concrete things or people we like and can see and touch, but how can we love the Invisible King? How can man love God? How are we to understand this verse of the Shema? The ancient sages of the Midrash discuss this question with commendable frankness. They did not try to gloss over the difficulties. They knew that the God they worshipped is the God of truth who does not want us to pretend to love Him when we do not. The ancient Midrash known as the Sifre, in a comment on our verse, says that the first verse of the Shema is followed by the injunction to teach the words to the children and to speak constantly of them. Thus the Sifre says: 'Take these words of the Torah to thy heart and in this way you will learn to recognize He at whose word the world came into being and you will cleave to His ways.'   T h i s highly significant statement is typical of the Rabbinic attitude to the religious life. Let us consider its implications. Men have found God through many different ways. Some have found Him through Nature and the intelligence manifest throughout Nature. Others have found Him through the pursuit of beauty. Others again have found Him in the stirrings of conscience in the human breast. Many have found Him in science's search for order and harmony in the universe. All these are, indeed, ways to God, yet the typically Jewish approach is to find God through the Torah, in the contemplation of His word. According to the Sifre there is nothing mystical or ecstatic about the command to love God, though these are undoubtedly present in other versions of Jewish teaching. The command is for Jews to study the Torah and practise the precepts of the Torah. By practising justice and showing mercy as enjoined by the Torah we are nearer to God. In this version of Judaism, it is not so much that the Torah leads to the love of God as that it *is* the love of God. There is much insight into the Jewish spirit in Renan's famous remark: 'To the Christian religion is his sweetheart, to the Jew it is his wedded wife.' It will not do to overstate the case. Other more mystical approaches are found in Judaism, as we have noted; but if one can speak of normative Judaism, the approach of the Sifre is that of normative Judaism.

47

Ekev

And thou shalt consider in thy heart, that, as a man chas-
teneth his son, so the Lord thy God chasteneth thee.
(Deuteronomy 8:5)

And now, Israel, what doth the Lord thy God require of
thee, but to fear the Lord thy God... (Deuteronomy 10:12)

And know ye this day; for I speak not with your children
that have not known, and that have not seen the chastise-
ment of the Lord your God... (Deuteronomy 11:2)

These three verses in our *sidra* have a common theme, the stern-
ness of God and the need to fear Him all as part of His compas-
sionate concern. The book of Deuteronomy is full of the love of
God, as noted in the comment on the previous *sidra*. In our *sidra*
Moses turns to the fear of God, equally important in the religious
life. In fact, the usual term for a religious attitude is *yirat
shamayim*, 'the fear of Heaven', and, as in English usage, the religious person is called a God-fearing man or woman.

There is, however, fear and fear. At the lowest level fear of God
means fear of what God will do: God's punishment that awaits the
sinner in this world and in the next, unless he repents of his wrongdoing while he still has the chance. The tendency in modern times
is to be uneasy about this kind of fear, which seems to treat God as
a tyrant ready to pounce or hurl thunderbolts. Yet even this kind of
fear – which is really more fear for one's own safety rather than fear
of God – can still be wholesome since frail human beings need the
spur to the good life it provides. The significance of this lower fear
is that it reassures us that evil does not permanently triumph and
evil men do not get away with it. All depends, however, on what is

meant by evil men in this context. If Hitler, to take the obvious example, had been afraid of God in this sense – if he had a real and ultimate terror of wrongdoing – the Holocaust might not have happened.

Most reasonable religious people are not afraid of fear even in this lower sense. The trouble arises when the religious extremists begin to invoke the notion of God's punishing people who are guilty of religious offences as if these extremists know God's providence in terms of a neat scheme of reward and punishment. Most of us are appalled when, say, some Rabbis try to explain the Holocaust as a punishment resulting from God's displeasure with the Jewish people, as if such horror can be understood in tit-for-tat terms. A number of Jewish thinkers in the middle ages explain the threat by God to withhold the rain and to bring about other calamities if the people fail to hearken to God's word, as a very simplistic warning to an immature slave people incapable of understanding what the Zohar calls the higher and true fear of God.

According to the Zohar, there are three types of fear. The first is the type mentioned above, in which a man is afraid to commit wrongs because he believes that God will punish him physically and materially – he will become sick or suffer heavy losses in business and so forth. At a more spiritual level is the second kind of fear in which a man is afraid that he will go to Hell, which the mystical writers such as the Zoharic authors understand in terms of spiritual anguish in the Hereafter as the absence of God, the result of sinfulness on earth. Yet Judaism does not normally place too much emphasis on Hell-fire, even of the metaphysical kind. According to the Zohar the highest form of fear is what Otto calls the numinous, the overwhelming sense of awe and dread in nearness to God. This is not at all fear of what God will do but the sense of dread leading to ecstasy at re moments in life but present, too, in a synagogue and other holy places.

THE SECOND SECTION OF THE SHEMA (DEUTERONOMY 11:13–21)

As early as the second century CE, the Mishnah calls this paragraph the second paragraph of the Shema, and it is recited in the liturgy together with the first paragraph and is written together with the first paragraph in the *tefillin* and the *mezuzah,* to which there are references in both passages. According to the Mishnah the first paragraph of the Shema constitutes the 'acceptance of the yoke of the Kingdom of Heaven' while the second paragraph constitutes 'acceptance of the yoke of the precepts'. The first paragraph is thus the general acceptance of the Jewish religion, called a 'yoke' because it naturally makes heavy demands on us, while the second paragraph enjoins acceptance of the detailed precepts of the Torah. To keep the precepts of the Torah without real religious belief is a form of behaviourism and simple ethnic habit; but to affirm acceptance of Judaism in general, without observance of the precepts, is very far removed from the actual practice of Judaism as a living faith. A non-Jewish writer has defined Judaism as the religion of doing the word of God. Very true; but Judaism is not mere behaviourism and its essential ingredient is the religious affirmation that makes it a religion at the heart of which is belief in the living God.

It can be seen easily that the first paragraph of the Shema is in the singular and is addressed to the individual: 'with all *thy* heart', while the second paragraph is in the plural and is addressed to the people as a whole. It has been suggested that this is why the first paragraph refers to 'with all thy heart, and with all thy soul, and with all thy might', while the second paragraph refers only to 'with all your heart, and with all your soul' but omits 'with all your might'. 'With all thy might' denotes extraordinary self-sacrifice and complete devotion and, while this is possible for rare individuals, it is unrealistic to expect such an attitude of people in general. For the same reason, it has been suggested, there is no promise of reward in the first paragraph of the Shema and there is promise of reward and threat of punishment in the second paragraph. This is because the individuals to whom the first paragraph refers are beyond reward and punishment and do God's will because of their love of God. The people as a whole, to whom the second paragraph refers, cannot be expected to do that which is right simply because it is right, and these are promised reward. As the Talmudic Rabbis say: 'Let a man study the Torah and practise the precepts even if his motivation has an element of self-seeking since out of the less than completely worthy motivation he will come eventually to the purest of motives.'

48

Re'eh

The verse in our *sidra*, 'Ye are children of the Lord your God' (Deuteronomy 14:1), implying that God can be described as a father, finds an echo in many a passage in the classical sources of Judaism. Not only in the Avinu Malkenu prayer, but in other passages in the liturgy, the paternal metaphor is used to denote the relationship between God and Israel. (It is worth noting in connection with feminism that, in one Biblical passage, at least, God's compassion is stated in terms of a mother rather a father: 'Like one whom his mother comforteth, so will I comfort you', Isaiah 66:13).

It is on record that, in medieval Germany, the knocker-up – the beadle who went around the houses to awaken people to come to the synagogue service in the morning – would first give one knock then two, then another one, standing for the letters *alef* and *bet*, one and two, and hence forming the word *abba* ('father'), as if to say: 'Rise up to serve Father.'

It is acknowledged by Christians that, when Jesus addressed God as 'Our Father who art in Heaven', he was not inventing a new designation, but simply using the current Jewish form – as, indeed, this appears in contemporary Jewish sources.

In the early sources of Judaism, the specially intimate relationship denoted by that of parent and child is reserved for God's relationship with the Jewish people, not with all mankind. Based on Chapter 10 of Genesis, it is better to speak of the cousinhood of man, all mankind enjoying a close family relationship, since all are descended from a common human stock. This is very different from thinking of all men as 'brothers', because they are the sons of the father, God.

To point this out is not to suggest that Judaism is not a universal religion. Judaism does teach that God has concern, as it were, for all His creatures, especially for the human race since every human being is created in the image of God. However this concept is understood, it certainly denotes a qualitative distinction of all human beings. Man resembles God in some manner impossible for other animals; and it is Judaism which teaches this. It is the message conveyed at the beginning of the creative narrative: 'And God created man in His own image, in the image of God created He him; male and female created He them' (Genesis 1:27). For all that, there is still a particularistic element in Judaism which, if ignored, proves detrimental to the faith.

As the great Rabbi Akiba put it long ago in *Ethics of the Fathers*: 'Beloved is man, because he was created in God's image.' Rabbi Akiba, however, goes on to say: 'Beloved is Israel, for they are called the children of God.'

> *Ye are the children of the Lord your God: ye shall not cut*
> *yourselves, nor make any baldness, between your eyes for*
> *the dead. For thou art a holy people unto the Lord thy God,*
> *and the Lord hath chosen thee to be His own treasure out*
> *of all peoples that are upon the face of the earth.*
> (Deuteronomy 14:1–2)

This section of our *sidra* records certain weird, idolatrous and horrible practices which were followed by worshippers of the pagan gods but which had to be utterly rejected by the 'children of the Lord thy God'. On the verse 'For thou art a holy people' the medieval Sefer Hasidim comments: 'Do not allow yourselves to be less holy than other peoples.' The meaning of this comment is that even when things legal in themselves are held to be obnoxious on moral and religious grounds to the adherents of other religions, Jews are to abstain from them in order not to allow the impression to be gained that adherents of the Jewish religion are less alert to the call of holy living than their non-Jewish associates. The Sefer Hasidim gives the example of an animal upon which bestiality had been committed. Religious non-Jews would never eat the meat of such an animal on moral grounds and since this is so, it is forbidden for Jews to eat that noisome meat even if the meat was otherwise rendered kosher by the act of *shehitah*. By the same token, a number of prominent Rabbis in the nineteenth century refused to allow a building that was a former brothel to be adapted into a synagogue or a precious dress donated by a notorious harlot to be used as a curtain to be placed in front of the Ark containing the

Scrolls of the Torah. When Rabbi David Hoffman was asked whether it is permitted for Jews to smoke in the synagogue, he replied that there was no actual, legal decision against it but, since Christians would not dream of smoking in a church, we Jews must not have standards lower than theirs. All this constitutes a grey area, one in which what is involved is not so much the actual law but good taste, a sense of what is fitting and a respect for the concept of holiness in general.

There is also a grey area with regard to the prohibition in our section on 'inquiring of the dead', usually translated as necromancy. But what exactly is involved in this prohibition and what is the reason behind it? The way the ancient Rabbis understand it, the prohibition is associated with idolatrous worship, both of the gods and of dead human beings who have become gods. Thus the whole realm of the dead was strongly associated with paganism, especially in the belief that supplicating the dead could have an effect for good or for ill.

In the middle ages, however, a distinction was drawn between asking of the dead body and contacting the soul. According to many medieval authorities it was the attempt to get in contact with the actual dead body, believed to have magical powers of its own, rather like the zombie of horror films. To attempt to get in touch with the soul of a person whose body has died is, according to some authorities, permitted; for example, if two men have promised one another that whichever one of them dies first will come to the other to inform him of what goes on 'up there'. Some even permit a living man to get in touch, if he can, with the soul of a dead person. Nevertheless, Rav Kook, in a famous Responsum, argued that while there is no technical or legal reason to forbid, say, a seance purely in order to satisfy one's curiosity or as an exercise in psychical research, and the experience may result in a greater and stronger belief in the supernatural, yet the Jews, as a holy people, should ideally be beyond attempts to strengthen their faith by such dubious means.

49

Shofetim

This *sidra* is part of the great legal code in Deuteronomy, the keynote of which is righteousness and justice in all human dealings. Addressed in the first instance mainly to judges, its demands were applied, wherever possible, to all Jews.

The injunction against taking bribes, for instance, has been applied in the Jewish tradition, not only to the judge who allows the gifts given to him to influence his decision, but to every Jew, who should not allow the prospect of personal gain to influence his pursuit of the truth.

At the beginning of the *sidra* the marvellous verse occurs: 'Justice, justice shalt thou follow.' The repetition of the word – *tzedek, tzedek tirdof* – suggests a passionate concern for justice, as if to say: 'Justice, only justice'. It is almost as if the Torah wishes us to be carried away so that every mention of the quality of justice summons forth a kind of fervent Amen.

On the face of it, passion is out of place in the area of justice. A subjective, emotional approach belongs more to art, music and literature than to the practice of righteousness. To be judicious would seem by definition to be objective, unemotional and dispassionate. But is it not in the decisions we are called upon to make when acting justly that fervour is required? The enthusiasm suggested in our verse refers rather to the joy with which the whole concept of justice is to be approached. It is possible and desirable to become excited by the very idea of justice.

Perhaps this notion can be properly grasped by those who have suffered through injustice, who know how much it hurts to be victims of oppression and exploitation. A sympathetic non-Jewish writer, C. S. Lewis, in the chapter in his book on the Psalms, entitled 'Sweeter than Honey', argues that the passionate heart of the Psalmist is moved by his suffering to long for a society based on the justice the Torah demands.

Witnessing the bitterness of injustice, the Psalmist longs to live in a society pervaded by the Torah ideals of justice. The Law, for him, is no cold, calculating, dry-as-dust discipline but sweeter than sweet, the very means to a worthy life in which men respect one another's rights and personality, even if they have not as yet attained to the higher ideal of loving one another.

> *Thou shalt not turn aside from the sentence which they*
> *shall declare to thee, to the right hand, nor to the left.*
> (Deuteronomy 27:11)

Originally referring to declarations by the judges belonging to the highest court in the land, this verse, in the post-Talmudic, Rabbinic period, was applied to the teachings of the Talmudic sages. Rashi, on the expression 'to the right hand, nor to the left', quotes the Rabbinic Midrash known as the Sifre to the effect: 'even if they [the sages] tell thee that thy right hand is thy left hand and thy left hand thy right'.

This has been understood by some commentators as demanding total obedience to the rulings of acknowledged authorities even when what they say is contrary to reason. Obedience is all, otherwise, it is argued, there could be no real authority at all. Even if the authorities tell you that which is forbidden is permitted and that which is permitted is forbidden, you must listen to them.

Others, however, interpret the Sifrea to mean: 'even if they *seem* to be teaching that right is wrong and wrong right', not where you know that what they say is untrue. On this understanding, a degree of individual autonomy is allowed. Both views have difficulties; in the one individual responsibility counts for naught; in the other, all authority is undermined. There is a wealth of discussion in the Rabbinic sources on this whole question and there are inevitable problems. Yet, on the whole, a working compromise has generally been adopted by Jews throughout the ages.

There is a pregnant comment by Bahya Ibn Pakudah, author of 'Duties of the Heart'. Bahya notes that our text refers to questions of law. Here authority must be upheld. In matters of belief and religious emotion, there cannot be an authority which regulates how a Jew should feel about his religion or what he should really believe deep down. As Solomon Schechter once said: 'You cannot get your father to write your love letters for you.' Such an attitude might have led to religious anarchy but, thanks to the good sense of Jews, it did not. Jews have been guided in purely religious matters by the mysterious consensus that prevailed in the Jewish community. Modern Jews can be inspired by Bahya's pertinent observation to enjoy a measure of independence while remaining loyal to what the community has decided, under God, to be the eternal truths of the Jewish religion.

50

Ki Tetze

That it may be well with thee, and that thou mayest pro-long thy days.　　　　　　　　　　　(Deuteronomy 22:7)

The reward for sending away the mother bird before taking the young is length of days. So, too, we are told, is the reward of honouring parents. The Talmud tells of a young man who, in obedience to the order of his father, climbed a lofty tree, sent away the mother bird before taking the young, but who fell on his way down and was killed. 'Where are the many days of life promised to the young man?' asks the sceptic.

The answer recorded in the Talmud in the name of the second-century teacher, Rabbi Jacob, is that the reward 'that it may be well with thee' refers to life in the World to Come, where all is well, and 'that thou mayest prolong thy days' refers to the World to Come, where there is life without end.

The whole doctrine of the Hereafter, the World to Come, as the Rabbis call it, has been held up to ridicule as base doctrine, mainly on two grounds. First, it is argued that the belief has been fostered by religious leaders with a vested interest in preserving the status quo in the social life of mankind. By directing the minds of their followers Heavenward, such leaders, it is claimed, effectively divert their attention from the social evils to be put right here on earth. Second, it is argued that the doctrine of the World to Come is a cowardly doctrine, the belief of a man too afraid to die. What is the Jewish answer to these criticisms?

As to the first, Judaism has never tired of reminding us that we acquire immortality by living the good life in this world, including our behaviour in endeavouring to make the world a better place in which people can live. Preoccupation with the material concerns of our fellows, observed a Jewish moralist, is not materialism but spirituality. A Hasidic master taught that God allows the possibility for human beings to doubt His existence, since if such doubting was impossible, the overwhelming tendency would be for men to leave all social betterment and all care to Him, and real human sympathy and compassion would be unknown.

Were not the great Hebrew prophets the pioneers of social concern in the name of God? And is not Talmudic legislation in such matters many hundreds of years in advance of its time? Does not the history of the Jewish community in the middle ages afford abundant evidence of the social conscience of the Jew? Evidently, the actors in the great drama of Jewish history found that having to play their role against the backcloth of eternity was no hindrance to achieving their goal.

As for the accusation of cowardice, those with insight into religious psychology know that the reverse is true. Belief in the Hereafter steeled countless men and women to lead good lives in the face of the most crushing odds. Were the martyrs, who were ready to give their lives for the faith, moral cowards?

The best and most authoritative Jewish teaching on this subject does not encourage us to look upon Heaven as a sort of spiritual bank in which we store our good deeds against a rainy day hoping for profitable dividends, but rather as a form of spiritual bliss and nearness to God, the striving for which ennobles our lives and refines our characters. Nothing can be more terrible and tragic than the feeling of futility which is bound to haunt the man who believes that 'at the end of days' this universe of ours will eventually run down and that all human dreams and achievements will ultimately vanish into nothingness. The man who lives under the shadow of eternity, however, measures his deeds in that light, and, by so doing, acquires a deeper sense of the abiding values as truly abiding.

> *When thou buildest a new house, then thou shalt make a para-*
> *pet for thy roof, that thou bring not blood upon thy house, if*
> *any man fall from thence.*   (Deuteronomy 22:8)

In Biblical times the roofs of houses were flat and people frequently walked on them, hence the injunction in our verse to construct a parapet around the roof. This had to be high enough to stop anyone falling off the edge of the unfenced roof. The Rabbis extend the rule of the parapet so as to cover anything that can be of danger, such as a vicious dog or a shaky ladder or, nowadays, an improperly serviced car or faulty electrical appliances.

The Hebrew for 'if any man fall from thence', *ki yippol ha-nofel mimmenu*, can be read as 'if the fallen one will fall from it', and this gives rise to the Rabbinic homily that the one who falls is the 'fallen one', i.e., the one destined to fall. This Rabbinic homily is grappling with the theological problem, of what use are precautions against accidental harm? If divine providence has decreed that a man fall victim to an accident then it is destined that the accident should happen. If, on the other hand, it had not been destined for the accident to happen, why the need for precaution? The implications of the Rabbinic answer appear to be that we live in a world in which accidents happen and, as resourceful and caring human beings, we are obliged to take all the necessary precautions against them happening. We must live as if we, and we alone, are responsible for whatever happens even accidentally, even while leaving the question to God why it happens to A rather than to B or, indeed, why it should happen at all. In the words of a Rabbinic saying: 'You do what it is your duty to do. The secret things of the All-merciful are not your concern.'

> An Ammonite or a Moabite shall not enter into the assembly of the Lord; even to the tenth generation shall none of them enter into the assembly of the Lord for ever.
> (Deuteronomy 23:4)

The Rabbis understood this verse to mean that an Ammonite or Moabite man, even after his conversion to Judaism, must not marry a Jewish woman, even though, once he has been converted, he is fully Jewish in every other respect. The law did not apply to a Ammonite or Moabite woman, witness Ruth, a native of Moab, who became the ancestress of none other than King David, as recorded at the end of the book of Ruth.

The Mishnah tells of one Judah, a convert from Ammon, who came before Rabban Gamaliel and Rabbi Joshua to ask whether he was allowed to marry a native Jewess. Rabban Gamaliel sought to apply our verse according to which Judah's marriage to a native Jewess was not allowed. However, Rabbi Joshua allowed him to marry on the grounds that Sennacharib 'confused all the nations', that is, by moving around the nations he had conquered as part of his political strategy. The original nations no longer reside in their land and it can be assumed that anyone who claims to belong to a particular nation does not really belong. As the Talmud elaborates it, the majority principle is invoked and the probability is that any particular person does not belong to the forbidden nations. Thus, whatever the intention of the original ban, the exclusion of certain peoples from marrying into the Jewish people was set aside; a revealing development in Jewish law, which demonstrates the flexibility adopted by the great Jewish teachers.

Ki Tavo

> *I have put away the hallowed things out of my house, and also have given them unto the Levite and unto the stranger, to the fatherless, and to the widow, according to all Thy commandments which Thou hast commanded me.*
> (Deuteronomy 26:13)

We are told in our text that at the end of three years, the farmer was obliged to see to it that all his tithes had been given: to the Levite (who had no land of his own), to the fatherless and the widow and, interestingly, also to the stranger, the non-Israelite who was poor. The poor man's tithe for the Israelite poor is enjoined elsewhere. At the end of these three years, the farmer had to make a solemn declaration, to which our text refers, that he had carried out his duties and in which he asks God to favour him.

The Rabbis call this declaration *viddui maaser*, 'confession of tithing'. A number of commentators find the expression 'confession' somewhat puzzling. Surely confession means acknowledgement that one has done wrong or failed to do right, but what meaning can be given to a declaration that one has done the right thing?

The answer is that a pat on one's own back, provided it is not overdone, can be salutary as a means of avoiding despondency and a lack of proper self-assessment. The farmer in Biblical times who carried out all his duties, difficult though these must have been, is entitled to a measure of self-congratulation in the presence of God; it is just as much an essential ingredient in his life of virtue as confession of his sins. Both are called 'confessions' because thy involve an introspective stance of honest assessment. Naturally, showing off to others is hardly to be commendable but, in our text, it is to God that the 'confession' is made and He knows the secrets of the heart.

Confession is no doubt good for the soul but there is a temptation among some religious people to acquire importance by treating the sins to which thy confess as of far greater significance than they really possess:

> Once in a saintly passion,
> I cried in desperate grief,
> O Lord, my heart is full of guile.
> Of sinners I am chief.
> Then stooped my ministering angel
> And whispered from behind:
> Vanity my little man,
> You're nothing of the kind.

The honest, rugged farmer in ancient times, with not the slightest pretension to saintliness, who is proud that he has fulfilled his obligations to others, comes far closer to God than the pseudo-pious man who fools himself that he stands out for his vices if he cannot stand out for his virtues.

There are a number of tales of Hasidic masters who, on their deathbed, instead of letting the Hasidim gathered around hear their confession of failure, preferred to let them hear how they declared to God at the end of their life that they had committed no major wrong and had led their flock on the right road to the best of their ability. A non-Hasidic boy, it is said, cheekily asked an old Rabbi why he did not weep bitterly during the formal confession on Yom Kippur. 'I have behaved properly during the past year', declared the Rabbi, 'and I have no cause to weep'.

> *And the Lord hath avouched thee this day to be His own*
> *treasure, as He hath promised thee, and that thou shouldest*
> *keep all His commandments.*   (Deuteronomy 26:18)

The Hebrew word translated as 'treasure' is *segullah*, a word that can certainly bear the meaning of a 'treasure' but has other meanings as well. One of the meanings of a *segullah* in the later literature is a remedy which works, say, a certain stone, though the reason why it works is a mystery. On this understanding of the word, there is an irrational element, a mystery, in the whole idea of the choice of Israel. On this view it is, indeed, odd of God to choose the Jews.

Another later meaning of *segullah* is a property that can be relied on never to decrease in value. For instance, the law states that guardians of the property of orphans who fear that it may decrease in value should buy instead on behalf of the orphans a *segullah*, that is, property that will suffer no serious decrease in value. Examples of a *segullah* in this connection are a precious stone or a Sefer Torah. According to this interpretation the Jewish people, with all its faults, can be relied on by God as a 'safe investment' who will never let Him down.

According to both interpretations, and they take us to the heart of the Chosen People idea, which obviously has its difficulties, there is an element of mystery in both God's choice of Israel and in His 'reliance', so to speak, on. And yet Jewish history has shown both that the choice works and that Jews remain loyal to the One who chose them. This approach is hardly rationalistic, but Jewish history and Jewish life have demonstrated that in this area it is not unreasonable for the religious Jew to continue to affirm the Chosen People idea.

> *And thou shalt write upon the stones all the words of this*
> *law very plainly.*   (Deuteronomy 27:8)

'Very plainly' means, according to a Rabbinic explanation, in seventy languages, i.e., in translation into all the languages on earth. This is no doubt an example of Rabbinic hyperbole, yet it contains a profound truth. Translation involves much more than putting thoughts expressed in one language into a different language so as to convey their meaning. When translated into a different language the thought itself changes as a result of the different cultural background of the language into which the original text is translated. The word Torah is a good example. When the Greek translators rendered Torah as *nomos* and were followed by the English translators rendering it 'Law', they were interpreting the whole concept into the thought patterns of the Greek-speaking Jews and English-speaking Christians with, on the one hand, an enlargement of the application of Torah so that it could find a lodging in the different languages, and a narrowing of the concept to its purely legal connotation.

This is why we find in the Jewish tradition a certain ambivalence on the question of Torah translations. There is both an approval of translation of the Torah, as here, and strong disapproval. Jews are now the heirs to both tendencies, which can be described as the universalistic versus the particularistic. Far from there being any harm in this, it can all be beneficial provided it is appreciated that all translation involves inevitably a measure of distortion of the original meaning as well as an uncovering of its wider meaning. Even a thoroughly Orthodox translation as the well-known Art Scroll, which claims always to be faithful only to the original text as understood in the Rabbinic tradition, is, in itself, a departure from the original simply because the language used in the translation is that of modern, American English.

52

Nitzavim

It is not in heaven. (Deuteronomy 30:12)

One of the most remarkable passages in religious literature is the Rabbinic story of the Sages who refused to obey a decision in Jewish law conveyed by a voice from Heaven. The Torah, they said, quoting our verse, is not in Heaven. It was given to the children of men who are obliged to grapple with its truths and apply them without divine assistance. The deeper meaning of this ancient tale is not that the heavenly voice spoke falsely but that it is irrelevant ÿo the religious needs of men, who require for their guidance a truth mediated through human reasoning.

There are three distinct attitudes with regard to the vexed question, debated for centuries, of the relationship between revelation and reason. At the one extreme are those who reject the whole idea of divine revelation. For them the Bible, great though it is, has been produced by humans with all the errors to which humans are prone and is no more 'inspired' than the works of Homer, Dante, Shakespeare and Milton are inspired.

At the opposite pole are those who dwell on the impotence of human reasoning to penetrate the veil of mystery surrounding the divine. This school argues that reason is a useful instrument for understanding the material and physical world. In this area, human reason applying scientific know-how has made tremendous discoveries and produced marvels of technological achievement; but in spiritual matters faith must reign supreme. How presumptuous of man to imagine that his puny mind can fathom the secrets of Infinity! Knowledge of God and His truth is possible only as a result of God's Self-Disclosure. It owes nothing to man, who is a purely passive recipient of the divine flow of grace.

The third view, behind such grand Jewish doctrines as that of the Oral Torah, which is developed in each generation and which never spends its creative powers, holds that the Torah is *from* Heaven but is not *in* Heaven. Divine though it is, the Torah was given through humans to humans. Its teachings are intended for real practical human situations. To appeal to a Heavenly voice now that the Torah has been given is futile, for the search for the will of God with man's limited but God-given mind is part of that will.

We live in a world grown suspicious of reason. Most of us today recognize the insufficiency of an ethical system that is not grounded in God; but though reason is prepared to yield to faith this must not be taken to mean that we can afford to believe anything we choose. No man willingly acts irrationally. Even the man who declares: 'Religion is a matter of faith not of reason' has, presumably, arrived at this conclusion by the exercise of his reason. Even a Nahman of Bratzlav, who maintained that God can never be found through reason since He is utterly beyond reason, still holds this to be a reasonable theological position.

'The Seder night is the time for asking questions', a young man inquiring about his religious problems was blandly told. Similar replies are all too prevalent. Unless we want our faith to deteriorate into superstition we must be prepared to allow reason the honoured place it once held in the Jewish tradition. As our *sidra* goes on to say: 'But the word is very nigh unto thee, in thy mouth, and in thy heart, that thou mayest do it.'

If one thinks about it, the whole concept of the divine revelation means that God, who is above all human comprehension, has conveyed to humans, through their reasoning powers, the significance of His word *for them*. We can obtain faint glimpses into how the supernal Torah, the Torah before God in Heaven, can exist independently of human beings, but such is not and cannot be the Torah we are obliged to follow. The ancient Sages who refused to allow even the Heavenly voice to dictate to them how they should interpret the Torah were surely right. Many lifetimes would be insufficient to explore the tremendous mystery; but we each have only our own lifetime to explore the significance and to apply its message for those whose destiny is to live in holiness on earth. 'That thou mayest do it', is the great teaching of the second verse quoted above.

Vayelekh

53

And Moses went and spoke these words unto all Israel.
(Deuteronomy 31:1)

The question that strikes the reader is, where did Moses go and where did he go from? The Greek translation known as the Septuagint seems to have had the reading: 'And Moses finished speaking these words', that is he finished the discourse in the previous passage. Evidently, the Septuagint read the Hebrew as: *vayekhal Moshe le-dabber'*, the very words which occur in a later verse (Deuteronomy 32:45), where the reference is to the words he had spoken previously. Interestingly enough, in a fragment found in Qumran this is the reading of our verse as well as of the later verse. It is easy to account for the substitution of *vayekhal* for *vayelekh* since both words have the same three letters – *vav, lamed, khaf* – though in a different order. A scribe could have written the word with the letters in a different order; scribes do make this kind of mistake accidentally when writing.

All this affords us an opportunity to consider the very complicated question of textual emendation of the sacred text of the Torah. Modern textual criticism departs from what had been the traditional view for many centuries: that our present text of the Pentateuch – the Masoretic Text – is the original text conveyed to Moses by God and that all variants found in the ancient versions such as the Septuagint are either simply wrong or are attempts to change the original text in order for it to make sense. The postulate of textual criticism is that, while the Masoretic Text is highly reliable and should generally be preferred to any other, there is no divine guarantee that the other versions are in error in all circumstances. Sometimes, at least, they preserve a better text. It is all a question of weighing up the different possibilities to see which are more probable.

There are still many Jewish teachers, all Orthodox teachers in fact, who would hold it to be heretical even to consider the possibility of textual emendation of the text sacred for so long and the one which appears in all the Sifrey Torah in the world. Many others, however, while not dreaming of altering the text in the Sefer Torah, would argue that this should not preclude the pursuit of scientific scholarship. It would, indeed, be sacrilegious to tamper with the text of all the Sifre Torah since, so far as living Judaism is concerned, it is the text as used for so many generations which constitutes the inerrant and supremely sacred text.

Such an approach, while incompatible with a doctrine of verbal inspiration, according to which the very words and letters of the Sefer Torah were divinely dictated, is certainly not incompatible with the doctrine that the precepts of the Torah, as understood by the consensus of the Jewish people, afford guidance from above to the people and through that people.

This diversion is more than a casual homily but should be seen as raising for devout Jews how textual (and for that matter historical) criticism can be given its head without this interfering with the acceptance that the Torah is ultimately the 'revealed word of God'. The rest is commentary, a commentary provided by the living and massive researches of both critical scholars and Jewish teachers throughout the ages.

> *Now therefore write ye this song for you, and teach thou it*
> *the children of Israel.* (Deuteronomy 31:19)

According to a very old tradition this verse constitutes the last of the precepts of the Torah and is the command for Jews to write a Sefer Torah. The medieval commentators, while seeing great value in each Jew actually writing a Sefer Torah (Maimonides did so), understand the implications to be that Jews should purchase sacred books in which words of Torah are recorded. Jewish learning is book learning and the Jewish people are the People of the Book.

According to the same tradition, the very first precept of the Torah is stated at the beginning of the creation narrative in Genesis: 'be fruitful and multiply'. Thus Jewish law rules that a man who owns a Sefer Torah should sell it only if he intends to use the money either to enable him to marry or to study the Torah. To sell a Sefer Torah for these two purposes is in itself to further the Torah ideal. The Torah can have no meaning unless it is studied assiduously and unless there are Jews who will engage in its study.

There has been much discussion on why the Torah is called here 'this song'. One important homily has it that the Torah is a great delight and should be studied as something infinitely more than as a bare, prosaic record. The Torah is a glorious song to be recited musically both literally (hence the traditional cantillation of the Torah) and metaphorically. Joy and melody are essential to every approach to the Torah and it is the music of the Torah that is the music of the spheres.

54

Haazinu

My doctrine shall drop as the rain. My speech shall distil
as the dew. (Deuteronomy 32:2)

In the Song *Haazinu* in our *sidra*, Moses compares his teaching to both rain and dew. In an agricultural society, the farmer prays for the rains to come 'in their due season', as expressed in the second paragraph of the Shema. When the rains fail, it is catastrophic, but it is also disastrous if they are too heavy, or are too prolonged beyond their season.

The gentle dew, on the other hand, is always welcome. As the Rabbis put it, rain is sometimes required and sometimes not, but the abundance of dew is required at all times.

Judaism is compared with both rain and dew. Like rain, it is needed on life's great occasions, the rites of passage – at birth, bar and bat mitzvah, marriage and death. On these occasions we confront the mystery of existence and are closer to the divine than at any other time.

The same applies to the special seasons of the Jewish year, to the feasts and fasts, each of them with its own distinguishing rituals. By these, Jewish life is redeemed from everyday banality and spiritual dryness. We all need periodic reminders of what we are, and the significance of our religion. That is, one imagines, why the Rabbis say that God is especially to be found during the ten days from Rosh Hashanah to Yom Kippur, and why the nineteenth-century Lithuanian moralist, Rabbi Israel Salanter, could say that the whole year should be like Ellul, the month of spiritual preparation before the ten days of penitence, yet Ellul should still be Ellul.

The comparison with dew represents the other aspect of Judaism – Judaism in the daily round, less spectacular than the

other aspect, but no less significant, the Judaism of honesty in business dealings; the Judaism of care for others; the Judaism of daily
prayer and benedictions; the Judaism of *kashrut*, in which even so
mundane an act as eating is brought into association with religion.
As the West London Synagogue's the Reverend Morris Joseph,
once said, when he heard someone deriding *kashrut* as 'kitchen
religion': 'It is better to have kitchen religion than drawing-room
irreligion.'

> *Remember the days of old, consider the years of many*
> *generations: ask thy father and he will declare unto thee;*
> *thy elders and they will tell thee.*   (Deuteronomy 32:7)

This verse was used by early Jewish historians as religious sanction
for the study of Jewish history. In modern times, under the
influence of the historical school, the study of Jewish history is
accepted as a most important branch of Jewish learning, without
which Judaism cannot be fully understood; some would add, or
understood at all. It was the contribution of the nineteenth-century
historical school, led by men like Zunz, Krochmal, Rapoport,
Frankel and Graetz, to demonstrate that Judaism is a historical and
developing religion. They showed that Judaism is a religion of
eternal truth, expressing itself in each age in accordance with the
spiritual needs and against the cultural background of that age.
According to the members of the historical school, if we 'remember
the days of old', if we recall and recapture our history, we learn to
understand the 'years of many generations', we recognize the
vitality of our religion and its rich variety of forms.

A Rabbinic Midrash comments on our verse as follows: 'Ask thy
father and he shall declare unto thee' refers to the prophets, who
are the fathers of the people. ' ... thy elders and they will tell thee'
refers to the post-Biblical sages of Israel. The Bible is the source of
Judaism but its teaching is worked out by the post-Biblical sages
whose activity is described from the Talmud, Midrash, the Jewish
philosophers, the preachers and teachers of Judaism down to the
present day. The members of each generation consult their
immediate elders and beyond them and in turn eventually become
elders themselves whom the next generation consults. If the link of
tradition is severed the result is anarchy.

A further Midrashic comment is pertinent. This Midrash notes
that the words *yemot olam*, translated as 'days of old', can mean

'days of eternity'. By pondering with understanding over the days of old we learn to recognize that ours is an eternal faith. By noticing how Jews grappled successfully with the problems of each age, we gain confidence in the power of Judaism to deal as adequately with the problems of the present. The study of Jewish history is of far more than antiquarian interest. Study of the Jewish past can provide us with the key to the Jewish future; or, as we say in the liturgy based on the Biblical verses combined: 'The Lord has reigned. The Lord reigns. The Lord will reign for ever and ever.' By understanding that God has reigned, that the finger of God can be observed writing in the past, we are moved to acknowledge Him in the present and to make sure that He will reign over us in the future.

> *For the portion of the Lord is His people.*
> (Deuteronomy 32:9)

The plain meaning of this verse is that the people belong to God. They are His portion, that which He has chosen. However, in some mystical tendencies, especially in the Hasidic version, Habad, the idea of God's portion is understood very radically to mean that there is a portion of God deep in the recesses of the Jewish psyche. Just as a tiny fragment of a diamond is a diamond character so the tiny fragment of God in the Jewish soul not only resembles God but is actually part of God.

We are on dangerous ground here. Many religious and mystical systems know of the idea of the divine spark in man, but it is generally assumed that, in Judaism, the abyss between God and man can never be crossed so that such an idea is incompatible with Judaism. Some would argue that this generalization is at fault. Habad is right that there is a spark of the Infinite in the Jewish psyche. This is limited to Jews since, according to this theory, as the result of the righteous patriarchs, the souls of their descendants are qualitatively different from the souls of other human beings. Many have found this idea of a qualitative difference between Jewish and Gentile souls highly offensive, though such an idea is found in Judah Halevi and some of the Kabbalists. Perhaps we should avoid speculation on such mysteries and be content with reading the verse in its plain meaning – so highly significant not to need to be buttressed by spiritual ideas, which far from assisting the spiritual quest are a hindrance to that quest.

55

Vezot Haberakhah

A man of Egypt delivered us. (Exodus 2:)
... Moses, the man of God ...
(Deuteronomy 33:1)

When the daughters of Jethro tell their father how Moses saved them from the shepherds, they describe him as an Egyptian. He wore Egyptian garb, he spoke the Egyptian language, his mode of thinking must have been influenced by the court circles in which he had moved since childhood. No one takes seriously, nowadays, the Freudian hypothesis that Moses was not a Hebrew at all but an Egyptian. However, Hebrew though he was, Moses in outlook and appearance must have been little different from the average Egyptian prince of his day.

The Midrash remarks that Moses begins his career as *a man of Egypt* but ends it as *a man of God.* The whole of Moses' life is the record of a struggle of a full-blooded, deeply impressionable man to shake himself free from the fetters of his background and, realizing the best that is in him, comes to see a new world-transforming truth.

The serenity of the wise man is not a divine gratuitous gift but the crowning reward of a life of inner tension during which the conflicts in his soul are resolved. 'When the fight begins within himself a man's worth something.' 'The greater the man,' teach the Rabbis, 'the greater his temptations.'

There is an old Jewish legend (though some, embarrassed by it, declare that it is a foreign importation), which tells of a painter sent by the King of Arabistan to paint Moses' portrait and bring it back to him. When the painter returned, the king had the portrait examined by his wise men, who pronounced it to be the picture of a cruel man, haughty, greedy for gain and possessed of a desire for power and by many vices. For, according to this legend, all these vices had been assigned to Moses by nature, but he struggled with them by long and intense efforts of the will until he overcame them.

A newspaper cartoon depicts a small boy, whose father had just read an adverse school report, saying to his parent, 'Well, Father, which is it, heredity or environment?' ' is one of the finest achievements of our age that we now understand the significance of a good family and background for the development of character and personality. Judaism, however, teaches that man is not a slave to his environment. He can rise above his handicaps or, better still, can use them for his moral advancement.

Moses was not a worse but a better leader of his people for having known at first hand the cruelties, the suave deceptions, the gross immoralities, and, one might add, the regal dignities of the Egyptian court. He was a worthier noble in the Kingdom of Heaven for having been brought up as an aristocrat in Pharaoh's palace. He was a stronger man of God for having been a man of Egypt.

'And there hath not arisen a prophet since in Israel like unto Moses', but the lesson of his struggle has much meaning for all Jews. For in our experience, too, there is that which corresponds to being 'a man of Egypt' and that which corresponds to being 'a man of God'. And thâe value of our lives depends, in large measure, on how successful we are in the long uphill climb from the one state to the other.

> Moses commanded us a Torah, an inheritance of the congregation of Jacob. (Deuteronomy 33:4)

A Midrashic comment on the word *morashah*, meaning 'inheritance', reads it as *meorasah*, 'betrothed bride'. What the Midrash is trying to convey is that to treat the Torah solely as an inheritance, as something precious that has come down to us from the past, is to preclude it from influencing our lives in a really vital way. The Torah should also be seen as the loving bride of Israel, which is why the man honoured to read the final verses of the Torah on Simhat Torah is called: 'The Bridegroom of the Torah'. *Hatan Torah*: an inheritance is ours without any effort on our behalf, unless we actively disown it. A bride has to be wooed. Love has to be shown to her and attempts made to pacify her when her displeasure is feared. In the metaphor of the Torah as Israel's bride lies all the tensions in the life of a couple intensely in love with one another. There are, at times, severe recriminations, tiffs and quarrels, and then love and making up. By the same token, we are called upon to love the Torah and, where necessary, where we cannot understand, for instance, to be irritated by her. And yet we know that our love for her can never be quenched.

The famous lecturer at the Rabbinical Seminary in Vienna in the last century, Dr Meir Friedman, gave a different turn to the idea of the Torah as Israel's bride. It is pleasant to own an inheritance, but such ownership can be no more than a source of pride. Unlike the bride–groom relationship it cannot be fruitful. This is the meaning of the Torah as Israel's bride, according to Dr Friedman. Throughout the ages, Jews have reflected deeply on the Torah and, as a result, have produced the comments without number, the children of the groom, Israel, and the bride, the Torah.

PART SEVEN
'ETHICS OF THE FATHERS'/*PIRKEY AVOT*

56

Ethics 1

He used to say ... (Ethics 1)

One of the most remarkable features of 'Ethics of the Fathers' (*Pirkey Avot*) is the variety of views expressed by the authorities recorded therein. Each one of the ancient teachers had his own particular approach to life's problems. The sayings transmitted under the formula: 'He used to say' are to be understood as the sum of each spiritual leader's *Weltanschauung*; his individual response to the challenges of his age.

These aphorisms represent the attempt of successive generations of teachers to sum up the message of Judaism in a manner relevant to the needs of the time, and in order to understand them correctly it is essential to see them in the light of the historical conditions that compelled their utterance. It will then be seen that the eternal message of Judaism offers a rich variety rather than a drab uniformity, that each age has its own application of Judaism and each teacher his own interpretation.

It is this variety which gives Judaism its peculiar strength. The representative thinkers and moulders of Jewish opinion had a love of originality as well as of conformity. Of each of them it is true that 'he used to say' – the point of view to which he gave expression had never before been given in precisely that way. The old wine, it was constantly being demonstrated, could be contained in new jars. The Jews of medieval Spain with their philosophical bent, their fondness for system and order, their wide mental horizons, produced a Maimonides; the Jews of France, with their profundity of Talmudic learning wedded to simple faith in the truth of tradition, produced a Rashi.

In this respect, Judaism is like great art. The paintings of a Rembrandt are quite different from those of a Constable; the works of both are far removed from the bronzes of an Epstein; but because the creations of all three are true to the rules, the observance of which can alone dignify them with the name of art, they are acknowledged as belonging to the most powerful productions of fertile imagination and superb skill.

The practice of Judaism, too, is an art. It is astonishing that people who would never dream of trying to paint without some basic training in the use of colour and form and in the use of perspective, or, for that matter, who would not dare to drive a car if they had not taken driving lessons, none the less imagine that Judaism can be understood without submission to any kind of discipline.

The truth is that Judaism demands such submission. All the great experts in the art of Jewish living have been prepared to make it; but compliance did not result in their case in a uniform characterization of their faith. Each of them produced, through the medium of their own soul, a fresh reading of the ancestral commitment.

The Rabbis have a penetrating comment on the verse in the first Psalm describing the activity of the student of the Torah: 'For his delight is in the Torah of the Lord and in His Torah doth he mediate day and night.' The personal pronoun in the second part of the verse, say the Rabbis, does not refer to God but to the student. When a man (nowadays one has to add or a woman) begins to study the Torah, they remark, it is as something external to him. Only after he has so assimilated its teachings that they have become part of his own soul does the Torah become *his* Torah – his own precious contribution which no one but he (or she) can make.

What a significant lesson for our time! Young people today are afraid that submission to the Torah will rob them of initiative and originality. They need not be. The Torah is a 'Torah of life' and like life itself custom cannot stale its infinite variety. Each Jewish man can so allow the Torah to influence his life that of him, too, it might be said: 'He used to say…'. And this, too, belongs to the Torah of our day with the innovative thrust that each Jewish woman can so allow the Torah to influence her life that of her, too, it might be said: 'She used to say…'.

57

Ethics 2

*An empty-headed man cannot be a sin-fearing man, nor
can an ignorant man be pious.* (Ethics 2:6)

A famous Jewish moralist was fond of saying that *yirat shamayim*,
'fear of Heaven', is an art and a science, requiring as much brain
power and application as the other academic disciplines. To
acquire the technique of living according to the Torah a man needs
qualities of mind as well as of heart.

This was the thought which the author of our text intended to
convey. He was not foolishly suggesting that we can afford to dis-
pense with emotion in our religion; this we cannot do, any more
than we can fall in love without the heart being involved. He did
believe, however, as did all the great teachers of Judaism, that you
cannot approximate to the Jewish ideal unless you are prepared to
drink deeply at the wells of Jewish learning, so that your faith is
based on sound thinking rather than on vague sentimentality.

It was not for nothing that the Rabbis elevated the duty of Torah
study to the status of a religious precept. They went further and
taught that it was the supreme religious obligation, one which
takes precedence over all others. There is no royal road to Judaism
or a Judaism without tears.

The only way to know what Judaism means is the hard way, the
way of effort and toil. 'If a man say to you,' declare the Rabbis, 'I
have not laboured but I have found [the Torah], do not believe
him', that is, do not believe him that he has found or do not believe
him that he has not laboured.

Nothing is more typical of Judaism than its love of learning. The
ancient Jewish elite, at least in Rabbinic times, was not recruited
by the standards of birth or wealth. Its aristocracy was one of

learning, its ranks cutting across all class divisions. Leading educa-
tors have come round to this point of view. Thomas Arnold's view,
which puts character before intelligence, is rejected by prominent
educationalists; or perhaps we ought not to say rejected, for
according to the Jewish view, the cultivation of the mind in the
pursuit of worthy aims helps to produce goodness and whole-
someness of character.

It is a distressing thought that few who call themselves intellectuals are loyal to traditional Judaism; but how many of them have
devoted any of their time to a serious study of our faith? They
would not dream of making solemn pronouncements on great
music without adequate training in musical appreciation. What a
pity it is that they feel competent calmly to weigh Judaism in the
balance and find it wanting without even embarking on the *sine
qua non* for the understanding of Judaism, a knowledge of the
Hebrew language.

It is an inspiring thought that one of the few Jewish intellectuals who had the honesty to examine Judaism before rejecting it,
Franz Rosenzweig, was so impressed by what he found that he
devoted the rest of his heroic life to the study and the practice of
the teachings of the Torah.

In a place where there are no men, strive to be a man.
(Ethics 2:6)

One interpretation of this well-known saying is that the Jew
should strive to live worthily even when no one will ever know of
it. God will know. Religion, Whitehead said, is what a man does
with his solitariness. It is not too difficult to lead the good life in the
full glare of the limelight. Even the best of men cannot help but feel
a glow of satisfaction when his virtue is recognized and lauded by
his fellows, though, as Adlai Stevenson said, this perfume should
not be inhaled. The real test of a man's goodness lies in its power
to grow and be nourished in secret. In a vital religious faith there
is bound to be an area in which man is alone with his God.

There is, however, another aspect of the virtuous life which
thrives on promulgation. Piety must not be permanently con-
cealed, otherwise the power of example is lost. Israel Salanter once
remarked that he was unable to understand the old Jewish legend
according to which there are thirty-six hidden saints in each generation in whose merit the whole world endures. When so much

has to be done for Judaism, he protested, how can the just afford to remain hidden? Righteousness must not only be done but must be seen to be done.

The saying is thus an appeal not to an ostentatious display of zeal but to a demonstration of goodness in action in order to serve as a stimulus to its emulation. When circumstances require the right deed to be done and there is no one else to do it, the Jew, conscious though he should be of his own spiritual inadequacy, must step into the breach. One of the most striking features in the lives of the great Hebrew prophets is their refusal to believe at first that the tremendous burden of prophecy was to be placed on their miserable shoulders. Once they became convinced that God had indeed spoken to them, however, they felt themselves compelled to speak in His name and even to defy the mightiest of earthly rulers if their mission required it.

On the deeper level, there is a sense in which this applies to all human beings. For no two men are exactly alike and Jewish teaching draws the conclusion that each person has a fraction of the divine light, as this has sometimes been put, which only he can reveal ... In the language of Jewish tradition, every man has his own 'portion in the Torah', his own individual interpretation of eternal truth, which will remain in concealment for ever unless he chooses to uncover it. 'Every man is obliged to say,' observe the Rabbis, 'for my sake the world was created.' In an age of totalitarianism, in which the individual is often in danger of being crushed out of existence, the authentic voice of religion urges men to serve God as individuals. No man should feel that he is a mere cog in the wheel. For if God can be said to need any man, He needs every man.

And be not wicked in thine own esteem. (Ethics 2:18)

We are often tempted to imagine that we are wicked. Our motives for this thinking may be varied, but chief among them is pride. We all hate to feel that we are commonplace; if we cannot be exceptionally virtuous, we are tempted out of vanity to imagine that we excel in wickedness. A further motive is laziness. It is so very attractive to avoid the difficult task of mending our characters, by convincing ourselves that we are too far gone for any attempts at moral improvement to have their effect.

That there is a need for genuine self-criticism no truly religious person would deny. The Rabbis have another saying which seems

to contradict the advice in our text, but which, if rightly understood, actually serves to supplement it. 'Always be wicked in thine
own eyes,' say the Rabbis, 'even if the whole world tells you that
you are a righteous man.' The seeming contradiction is easily
resolved if we note that the Hebrew word *beatzmekha*, translated as
'in thine own esteem', really means in thine essence or in thy self.
The objection is only to the false self-condemnation which seeks to
persuade us that we are so thoroughly bad that no improvement
is possible; the attitude of 'God made me as I am, there is nothing
to be done about it'.

This adjustment of ourselves is required not only in the life of
the individual but also in the life of a group and a people. No
people can succeed in strengthening the moral and spiritual aims
of its life as a particular people without constant, unflattering
introspection and without unflinchingly laying bare any evils in its
group life. The Jewish people, with a profound realization of the
importance of dissatisfaction with its spiritual attainments as a
preliminary to repentance, has year by year during the penitential
season described itself in its prayers as a sinful people.

The Bible never seeks to hide the sins of the people of Israel.
The great prophets set their faces against evils in the national
polity wherever they found them. One of the greatest factors in
the miraculous survival of the Jewish people is its genius for
uncovering its faults and not condoning its own shortcomings.

Yet, as in the case of the individual, the case of the Jews who are
never happier than when they are demonstrating that we are all
bad, has its obverse side. Constant reiteration of guilt often had the
effect of paralysing any effort to improve the lot of the Jews. Too
often Jews acquired such a deep-seated feeling of inferiority that
they were ready to believe as true the foulest lies which the distorted imagination of the anti-Semite invented about them. No
national revival was possible as long as this attitude prevailed, and
it is to the eternal credit of the Zionist pioneers that they shook the
Jewish people out of their apathy and taught them self-reliance.

Nowadays we have with us two kinds of Jews, both having the
wrong attitude to Jewish self-criticism. There are those who would
claim on behalf of Jews, especially after the Holocaust, immunity
from any kind of criticism, branding as a traitor to his people any
Jew who offers it. That such an attitude is untrue to the Jewish
tradition is patently obvious.

We also have the prophets of woe, who see us all as miserable sinners with no merits of our own, existing solely on the merits of our righteous ancestors. Such people would deny our generation the right to undertake any important work of spiritual reconstruction. Any new idea is rejected out of hand on the ground that we, in relation to the giants of the past, are pygmies and the argument is dismissed that a pygmy standing on the shoulders of a giant can see farther than the giant. No people can ultimately lead a healthy life if constantly tortured by feelings of guilt. The message of our text is directed against such critics: 'Be not wicked in thine own esteem.'

> *It is not thy duty to complete the work but neither art thou*
> *free to desist from it ...*   (Ethics 2:21)

A sense of proportion is one of the most difficult things to acquire. The either/or attitude to which a man is driven by his sense of consistency is particularly present in matters of religion.

The religious person finds it hard not to follow his ideals to what seems to him to be their logical conclusion. For him there are no half-measures. He has seen a vision and it must be brought to fruition; convinced that he is on the right path he must persist in it until he reaches his goal. This is the strength of the religious mind. It is also its weakness. For it is given to few men to witness the complete realization of their dreams and ambitions and a perfectionist policy is all too frequently self-defeating.

Religious assurance is one of the most powerful spurs to action, but, paradoxically, such assurance can sap our energies. We feel that nothing but the best is good enough for God so that where our efforts fail to produce the best we tend to refrain entirely from action. Our faith becomes quietistic. We adopt a passive attitude to life and its strivings. Such a view is, however, basically irreligious. It assumes that man is self-sufficient. It fails to appreciate that even our best is not an adequate return for God's love. It is too confident that God's purposes can be fulfilled only through our puny efforts. Chesterton's inversion of the popular proverb: 'If a thing is worth doing it is worth doing badly', is a sane view of human capacities for service. It must also not be forgotten that the most bizarre and horrible manifestations of the religious spirit such as unbridled and life-hating asceticism and the flight from reason have been the result of uncontrolled zeal wedded to unyielding logic. Solomon Schechter's observation that the best theology is not consistent probably has something of this in mind.

The true religious attitude would seem to be that God has given us work to *do*, not to *complete*. The task of Moses was done even though he was not permitted to enter the Promised Land. For Moses to have completed the work would have left no room for Joshua and God needs a Joshua, as well as a Moses.

The ideal attitude to our life's work is one which avoids the extremes of both complacency and over-earnestness. That God *helps* those who do His work is sound Jewish teaching. This implies, on the one hand, that we do not calmly sit back and leave the issue to Him without personal commitment to the work, and, on the other hand, it implies that we do not become so obsessed with the will to achieve that we leave Him out of our schemes.

We are God's instruments and it is our glorious privilege to be used in His service; even if the goal for which we strive is barely perceived, we are content to leave the question of purpose to Him. In this consists the wisdom of the ancient sage who taught: 'It is not thy duty to complete the work, but neither art thou free to desist from it.'

58

Ethics 3

Everything is foreseen, yet freedom of choice is given.
(Ethics 3:9)

Judaism, it has frequently been said, is a reasonable faith. It offers no affront to the rational side of man. It demands no belief in the impossible, refusing to elevate the absurd by calling it a divine paradox. All this is largely true – though the history of Jewish thought has thrown up a number of distinguished anti-rationalists – and yet Judaism also knows of the inexplicable element in religious faith.

While Judaism is not a faith opposed to reason, it does teach that there are areas into which reason cannot penetrate. Man with his finite mind cannot hope to comprehend the nature of God. 'For My thoughts are not your thoughts, neither are your ways My ways, saith the Lord.' A perennial problem, beyond the scope of human reason to solve, is the reconciliation of divine foreknowledge with human freedom.

The difficulty has often been stated. If God knows beforehand all that will happen, how can man be free to choose? If, for instance, God knew, long before either was born, that Hitler would bring destruction upon millions of innocent people and that Churchill would defeat him and help to rid the world of Nazism, how can Hitler be blamed for his atrocities and how can Churchill deserve any credit for his courage and steadfastness in the face of evil?

Some thinkers have sensed the dilemma so acutely that they have felt obliged to deny God's complete knowledge of the future in order to preserve the belief in human freedom. Others have denied that man is entirely free and have favoured a deterministic view of human existence. In the broad tradition of Judaism neither alternative is satisfactory.

In some way, many Jewish thinkers have argued, God's fore-knowledge is not incompatible with human freedom. We can obtain brief glimpses of how this may be possible. There are times, at least, when we can appreciate the idea that God is outside the time process altogether and that He sees, as it were, past, present and future 'all at once'. As C. S. Lewis once said: 'There are no tenses in God.' When all has been said, however, we recognize that we are in the presence of a mystery, and this is as it should be. If our faith were perfectly intelligible in all its details it would certainly be false, for it would then be purely human. The great Hasidic thinker, Nahman of Bratzlav, went so far as to say that unless the man of faith has doubts then whatever he believes in, it is not God. The man of faith, then, seizes both horns of the dilemma. He believes in God's foreknowledge and yet is convinced that, albeit within limits, he has freedom of choice.

Rabbi Akiba appears to be the author of our saying since it appears in the context of other sayings of the great Rabbi. Akiba was a man born into a family in which learning counted for nothing, who educated himself until he became the supreme master of Jewish learning. A man who refused to be daunted by the might of Rome and who persisted in teaching the Torah in spite of the Roman edict forbidding such activity. A martyr whose death, according to the legend, caused the very angels in Heaven to protest: 'Is this the reward of the Torah?' 'Such a one became a man of destiny because he had emancipated himself from the chains of destiny. Akiba was speaking from the fullness of his own experience and with the authentic voice of Judaism when he proclaimed: 'Everything is foreseen yet freedom of choice is given.'

> *He used to say, he to whom the spirit of his fellow-creatures takes delight, in him the Spirit of the All-present takes delight; and he in whom the spirit of his fellow-creatures takes not delight, in him the Spirit of the All-present takes not delight.* (Ethics 3:13)

This teaching of Rabbi Haninah, seeming as it does to prefer popularity over integrity, is strange. As Dr Hertz remarks, if taken at its face value it does scant justice to the prophet or the martyr; human favour does not, as a rule, shadow them. The tag *vox populi, vox Dei* has often had pernicious results when applied to life's problems; its contradiction is advocated by the pungent Yiddish saying *olam-golem*, 'the public is a stupid clod'.

One of the besetting sins of our age is the cult of glorification of personality without reference to the character it conceals. A pleasant manner, a pleasing exterior, courteous behaviour and a good measure of the social graces – these are sufficient to cover a multitude of sins. The inevitable result of such stress on external virtues is to leave a door wide open through which the demagogue can all too easily capture the public heart and mind.

This can hardly be the Jewish ideal. It was no doubt in opposition to the facile assumption that popularity is evidence of good character and sound leadership, that a Talmudic teacher observed: 'If a scholar is liked by his townsfolk it is not because he is worthy, but because he has failed to rebuke them for their religious and moral shortcomings.' What, then, did Rabbi Haninah mean?

The answer is to be found in the words of our text, *nohah hayemenu*, generally translated as 'takes delight in him' but actually meaning 'at ease with him'. There is no suggestion here that it is right to pander to the vulgar taste, still less of requiring the sanction of the ignorant as to the validity of our religious views. The lesson conveyed here is that the course we adopt in our religious life must not be of such a nature as to repel ordinary people who have a wholesome, common-sense outlook. The way of life we adopt, says Rabbi Haninah, should be such that even those who cannot accept it can still be 'at ease' in its presence.

The truth of the matter is that while the prophet and the martyr may forfeit the love of their fellows by their stern, unrelenting insistence on obedience to the call of duty, they do, none the less, evoke feelings of profound respect, even in the hearts of those who are prepared to stop at nothing in order to prevent their voice being heard. The message of the prophet and the martyr, and, one might say, of the exceedingly good man, makes us lesser mortals very uncomfortable. If we are honest we often dislike figures who challenge us to be as they are or, at least, to be better than we are. Our very struggle against such persons often arises out of a tacit recognition of the truth of their message. Not so the disturbance created by the fanatic, the bigot, the crank. Those who repudiate their ideas do so with righteous indignation at the affront to human personality of these misguided folk's confusion between enthusiasm and conviction and their conversion of a side issue into a main issue.

Religious people tend to be one-sided. Their faith can be of that narrow, bitter variety which few can respect and fewer still admire. It was against this cramping conception of religious faith that Rabbi Haninah preached. The same thought has often been voiced in subsequent Jewish teaching. It was well expressed by the Hasidic master, Menahem Mendel of Kotzk, who paraphrased the verse: Ye shall be holy men unto Me' to mean that the ideal of holiness ought not to produce an inhuman type of personality. 'Be holy,' said the Kotzker, 'but at the same time be a mensch.

And receive all men with cheerfulness. (Ethics 3:16)

Religion is concerned with the little as well as with the great things. It teaches that God is not only to be seen on the mountains but He reveals Himself in the valleys. It recognizes the value of the kindly smile, the encouraging word, the friendly gesture, the token of sympathy, the human touch. Rabbi Ishmael was one of the most famous of the Talmudic Rabbis. His views on Judaism have guided Jews throughout the ages, and yet of all his profound maxims it was this one that the editor of the Mishnah saw fit to record: 'Receive all men with cheerfulness.' The saying is even more significant in that it comes from a prominent member of the priestly aristocracy of ancient Judea.

Virtue and good cheer do not always go hand in hand. The notorious condemnatory Puritan conscience is more than a malicious invention of the sceptic. Some devout people, harsh on themselves, have little room in their hearts for the simple human joys. The long face can be the badge of charmless sanctity.

The Hasidic movement in particular placed great stress on the role of joy in the religious life. It has to be appreciated that the Hasidic doctrine of joy is basically a mystical virtue, with the mind constantly on God. Yet Hasidism also knows of the simpler form of sheer delight by companions in each other's company, which partly explains the phenomenal success of the movement during the eighteenth century. At that time in Eastern Europe, when oppressive governmental regulations as well as abject poverty combined to make it hard to be a Jew, ordinary men and women needed desperately the assurance that they counted in God's eyes, that they could rejoice in Him and He in them. As it has been said, Hasidism afforded mysticism for the masses. The Hasidic doctrine of the Zaddik as God's representative on earth was no doubt theologically objectionable, but the welcoming smile of the master and even his 'holy rages' persuaded his followers that they had significance in themselves and were more than mere figures in a communal register and useful drudges to help increase communal revenues. 'God dislikes melancholy and depressed spirits,' taught Nahman of Bratzlav. 'It is the duty of the joyful person to endeavour to bring to those in sadness a portion of his mood.'

It hardly needs saying that, when the Jewish masters spoke of joy, they were motivated by higher feelings than the desire to 'win friends and influence people'. No one can have much respect for the insincere 'back-slapper' or the religionist with a cheery 'unholier than thou' attitude. The Jewish teachers stressed the value of joy in their realization that the man of faith must delight in the fact that God cares for His creatures and wants them to care for one another.

How much human misery could be averted if only Rabbi Ishmael's lesson were taken to heart! It is a pity that our fear of sentimentality inhibits us from saying the right word when it is needed; the loving word between husband and wife; the word of confidence and trust between parents and children; the word of appreciation for work well done from employer to employee; the word of teacher to the promising and even to the not so promising pupil. There is little that is spectacular in these things but the God we worship is the God who first appeared to Moses in the lowly bush that was afire with Him. This is why Rabbi Ishmael advises that every man be received with cheerfulness and why we are told that Rabban Johanan ben Zakkai would greet every man he met in the market-place with the greeting of Shalom, even if those he met were pagans. They, too, were human beings created in God's image.

59

Ethics 4

Ben Zoma said:...Who is rich? He who rejoices in his portion.   (Ethics 4:1)

Ben Zoma's famous aphorism is not aimed against ambition as such. Provided that a man's aspirations are directed towards social aims, provided that, in his eagerness for a better and richer life, he does not use others as pawns in a selfish game of his own, a man's ambitions may be innocent, and may even be a force for good. Ben Zoma does not advise a man to be satisfied with his portion but to rejoice in it, quite a different thing. There is a certain kind of restlessness, a divine discontent with present conditions and a longing to bring about a better state of affairs, without which all progress would be impossible.

What Ben Zoma does counsel is the cultivation of the serenity of mind that enables a man to take the trials and tribulations of life in his stride, to face disappointments and misfortunes philosophically and avoid feeling frustrated when the world does not give him what he imagines to be his due. This teaching was finely underlined by the thirteenth-century teacher, Jacob Anatoli, who, preaching the wisdom of contentment, said: 'If a man cannot get what he wants, he ought to want what he can get.'

Is this a counsel of perfection? Is it really possible for a man so to attune himself to life that he can face all its vicissitudes with equanimity? Ben Zoma gives the answer: 'He who rejoices in his portion' (*behelko*). The man who believes that his life is a God-given portion, who believes, with the Rabbis, that no man can ever touch that which is destined for his neighbour, that man can eventually discover the blessing of tranquillity. The ideal Jew faces life's misfortunes, not in stoical indifference to them, nor as the man of so little faith that his sufferings bring him to despair, but as the pious man in the Talmud who was able to declare: 'Whatever God does is for the best.' Ben Zoma is careful, however, to say: 'He who rejoices in *his* portion'. If contentment is a virtue when applied to ourselves, it becomes a vice when exercised on behalf of others. Even if we are great enough meekly to accept our own sufferings, we ought never to remain unmoved at the contemplation of the miseries of other human beings. The Jewish ideal is that of Moses, who wore himself out with the burden of his people, who in his bold pleading dared the wrath of the Almighty Himself.

We ought first, taught a nineteenth-century Jewish moralist, to be concerned with the material lot of others. Next we ought to show discontent with our spiritual life. Then we can express dissatisfaction with our own lack of success in material things. Only then, and even so rarely, are we justified in being discontented with the spiritual attainment of others.

Yet the need for contentment does not apply only to our material portion in life. The Hasidim, with deep insight into the psychology of the religious life, taught that for a man to find peace of mind he must learn to have patience in his desire to storm the citadel of spiritual and intellectual attainments. While a man should strive to better himself spiritually and morally, as well as for intellectual prowess, he must be aware of his limitations and not attempt the impossible. Each person has his own ladder to heaven, his own sphere of endeavour, determined by his environment, his native talents and many other factors, beyond which he cannot go but within which he can achieve greatness. Some Hasidic masters even question the need to achieve greatness, in their belief that man's task is to do his best without thinking of spiritual ambitions. Acceptance of this with joy is what Ben Zoma advises. The way to mental health is to adopt Ben Zoma's counsel and rejoice in our God-given share of the precious gift of life.

> Ben Azai said: Despise not any man and carp not at any thing; for there is not a man who has not his hour and there is not a thing that has not its place. (Ethics 4:3)

Ben Azai teaches here that every human being created in God's image has a special dignity and a special role to play in God's world.

Most people seem to believe that the great man is preoccupied with great deeds and tends to cultivate the society of outstanding personalities. The truly great, however, are capable of finding significance even in the apparently trivial; because of this we have some delightful stories of how great Jews in the past were concerned to protect the dignity of their fellows. The famed Rabbi Nathan Finkel of Slabodka was once observed reciting the Kaddish in the synagogue and making a number of mistakes in the Aramaic. His puzzled disciples later discovered that he did this in order not to embarrass an elderly man who had previously recited the Kaddish with mistakes.

Rabbi Finkel's teacher, Rabbi Israel Salanter, once found that the poor-house in Kovno was in a state of extremely bad repair. The poor unfortunates were obliged to sleep in the cold and squalor without anyone doing much to improve the situation. Whereupon Rabbi Israel left his comfortable home to sleep in the poor-house himself, refusing to leave until the community collected sufficient funds to make the improvements.

These men were not shallow sentimentalists. When the situation demanded it, they could be stern and even severe. They saw, however, the great truth that no human being can assess correctly the value of any other in the eyes of God and that, therefore, the proper attitude was to find constant excuses for others, none for oneself.

The constant references by the authors of the Jewish moralistic literature to their own unworthiness are not to be seen as a kind of morbid self-delusion. Only a fool fails to recognize his own good qualities, and yet anyone who has ever tried to achieve the difficult task of self-improvement knows the perversity of human nature and becomes increasingly conscious of his faults. This can sometimes lead to an attitude which gives up in despair.

It can, however, lead to a very different approach to life. One's own weaknesses become the means of cultivating sympathy and understanding for the trials and errors of others who, for all we know to the contrary, may be making a greater moral success of their lives.

The Golden Rule in the Book of Leviticus (19:18) is followed with the words: 'I am the Lord'. For a person who acknowledges that God rules and has a plan and a purpose for every single one of His creatures, even the most apparently insignificant, will be inspired to pay proper respect to their needs, their strivings and their personalities. Such a person of faith, as Ben Azai said, will never despise any man as basically inferior to himself.

> *Rabbi Yannai said: It is not in our power to explain either the prosperity of the wicked or the afflictions of the righteous.* (Ethics 4:)

The problem of pain, of why the wicked prosper and the righteous meet with adversity, is the most stubborn obstacle to a theistic faith. Even Moses, according to the sages, failed to pierce the veil.

Rabbi. Yannai frankly admits that there is no final solution to this problem capable of being grasped by the human mind. Only the Infinite can comprehend the Infinite. Man, with his finite human mind, can see, at the most, only a tiny fragment of the truth. How, then, can he hope to understand the mysterious way in which God moves? 'If I knew Him I would be He,' wrote a great Jewish thinker long ago.

Yet Rabbi Yannai's admission of incompetence is not scepticism or agnosticism, still less is it stoical indifference to human suffering. It is rather an optimistic affirmation that, difficult though it may be to believe, there is a plan and the purpose behind the riddle of human existence. Somehow, suggests Rabbi Yannai, it does make sense. The solution is not in our hands, we cannot understand it; but there is a solution. We are not at the mercy of blind forces, but the creatures of a benevolent God.

The complete solution of the problem of pain has not been revealed to man. Yet there are certain considerations which are of help to us when we are confronted by the burning problem. The first of these is that our distress at the problem is in itself part of the solution. Precisely because the good in us refuses to tolerate the evil in creation, we are strengthened in our faith in a benevolent Creator. For if the universe really is the product of blind chance, then where, and how, did we acquire our sense of dissatisfaction with it? Where and how did we, as part of the universe, learn to view it from the outside to pronounce that certain of its features are good, others evil? With a belief in God you are faced with the problem of evil. Without belief in God you are faced with a problem every bit as stubborn – the existence of the good.

There is the further thought. God must allow men to do evil if they are to be given freedom of choice to do good. For if every time a man wanted to wrong his neighbour God forcibly restrained him, then man would be compelled to do good, seeing that he could then do no other. It is a terrible thing to contemplate that God allowed the Nazis to murder six million Jews, but if man were incapable of using science to build gas chambers, there would be no merit in using science to promote human happiness and well-being.

Of course God could have created man perfect, without the power to do evil, but evidently God does not choose to be worshipped by automatons, compelled to be good, but by human beings who freely choose the good. Also, if God had created automatons who had to be good by their very nature, what meaning would there be to the 'good' they do? Since they could not do otherwise, to call them good would be akin to ascribing moral sense to a machine.

It is the teaching of Judaism that, difficult though it may be to understand the purpose of pain and suffering, God desires that man should overcome them, working, as is implied by the Rabbinic teaching, in co-operation with his Divine Creator. The world has no use for a religious faith that bids its adherents to view life through rose-coloured spectacles, oblivious to the evil in the universe; but it also has no use for a faith which passively accepts suffering as the inevitable and unyielding fate of mankind.

Judaism recognizes that life is often brutal, dangerous, nasty, grim and insufferable; but it is an optimistic faith, none the less, not in any facile sense, but in the sense that it believes man is capable of working with God in the struggle against evil until the time comes when evil and pain will be vanquished. Then the good will prevail, but it will be a good earned by man with the help of his Maker.

60

Ethics 5

What is thine is thine and what is mine is thine, is a saint.
(Ethics 5:13)

According to this ancient teaching, the saint (*hasid*) is the man who is always ready to give his wealth, his talents, and his energy, to other human beings and to God, without thought of payment for his services. The saint, far from anticipating favours from the recipients of his benevolence, positively rejects the gifts of others. He desires no payment of its debts from a world owing much to him for his efforts on its behalf. Is such a person a real saint or is he simply daft, as the cynic would say?

The word *hesed*, from which the word *hasid* is derived, expresses a greater degree of unselfishness than the parallel word *tzedakah*, the word generally used for charity. The impulse to give charity acquires its strength from contemplation of the needs of others and the appreciation of the duty of satisfying those needs. The impulse towards *hesed*, towards benevolence, however, comes from within and is an expression of that deeper urge which makes the saintly person feel that his personality is incomplete and unfinished if he does not constantly occupy himself with good deeds, or, at least, that is the saintly ideal put forward in our text, one hardly realizable for most of us unless we are deluding ourselves.

This thought was so real to the Jewish mystics that they made use of it to solve one of the most difficult theological problems. Why, it is asked, did God create man? The usual answer, in order for man to enjoy eternal bliss, the mystics found unsatisfactory, since, they argue, if man had not been created, he would not have been in existence to experience either bliss or deprivation. The

answer the mystics give is that God is the source of all benevolence. The desire or the will to benefit those outside His Being is
part of His nature, if one dare speak of it in this way. Man
therefore had to be created as the object of God's bounty, so that
God, in Tennyson's words, could 'fulfil Himself in many ways'. The
lesson the mystics derive from this is that when man has developed the ideal of disinterested service he is truly Godlike.

The cynic again maintains that even the saint thinks only of
himself since it is saintly conduct that he wants for himself. The
cynic would say that when the saint declares: 'What is thine is
thine and what is mine is thine', he, too, adopts a self-serving attitude and is really saying: 'What is thine is mine', since he is using
the other for his own values. Such an attitude, however, overlooks
the fact that human beings have altruistic instincts, to exercise
which belongs to the nature implanted in them by God. In addition to our natural grasping nature, which says: 'What is thine is
mine and what is mine is mine' and to which we yield at times,
there is the other side of our nature according to which, at other
times, we can be unselfish and even 'saintly'. Our text is best seen
as an assessment of human nature at its best.

> Ben Bag Bag said 'Turn it [the Torah] and turn it over
> again, for everything is in it.'   (Ethics 5:25)

It is told of the Caliph Omar that when the great library in
Alexandria was burning he refused to let the flames be put out, for,
he argued, if the contents of the books were in accordance with the
Koran, they were redundant, and if they contained teachings not
found in the Koran, the books were false and deserved to be burnt.

Any religious system with a claim to exclusiveness is faced with
the problem of either assimilating or rejecting new knowledge not
found in its sacred scriptures. In a situation where the new
clamours for recognition by adherents of the old, two attitudes are
possible. One is that of the Caliph Omar, which most reasonable
religious people consider to be too narrow and too inhospitable to
new truths. The other recognizes that the new truth, by helping
people to acquire a deeper understanding of the old, may be
neither redundant nor false.

Judaism has not been free from this dilemma. There have not
been lacking in the past, and there are still to be found in the
present, Jewish thinkers who favour a narrowing down of the

legitimate scope of Jewish studies, quoting Ben Bag Bag's maxim as their authority. For such teachers it is inconceivable that the non-Jewish world has anything to teach us in matters of religion and morals. For them the Higher Criticism, for instance, or the study of comparative religion and philosophy, unless from the works of devout Jews, is completely false and should be taboo.

The life of a man like Maimonides provides us with a corrective to this limited view. For him all truth is from God and has to be accepted from whichever source it comes to humans. According to this giant of broader views, the study of the physical sciences could be included under the heading of study of the Torah because it enlarged man's horizons to perceive the harmony, beauty and wisdom exhibited in the world God has created. Similarly, this great Jew was, in a sense, the founder of the science of comparative religion by showing that the Bible could be really understood only against its ancient Semitic background.

Can there be any doubt which of the two methods is valid today? The supposed conflict between science and religion does not bother many people any longer, it being widely appreciated that science and religion belong to different categories and there is no real discord between the two. However, if Maimonides's idea is acceptable, science itself can be a religious exercise in that through it our awe of the majesty of nature leads to the reverence for the Creator.

'What know they of England who only England know?' Our faith has always been enriched by thinkers who approach it from without as well as from within or, rather, by approaching it from without as well as from within, the 'within' itself acquires a deeper and richer understanding. 'Turn the Torah over and again', implies Ben Bag Bag, and you will come to appreciate that 'everything is in it'.